D0267710

Community Learning & Libraries
Cymuned Ddysgu a Llyfrgelloedd

Newport
CITY COUNCIL
CYNGOR DINAS
Casnewydd

This item should be returned or renewed by the
last date stamped below.

CAERLEON

2 2 SEP 2015

0 2 MAY 2017

26 JUN 2017

DISCARDED
fro...

1 7 FEB 2018

To renew visit:

www.newport.gov.uk/libraries

THE MAN WHO KILLED RICHARD III

Lead the van, party of Urien,
We are waiting for leaders;
Raise your splendid ancient banner,
Your ravens, and rout the Saxons;
Lead man, in one course
With the tamed ravens of the son of Urien of old.
Hywel ap Dafydd ap Ieuan ap Rhys (1450–80)

THE MAN WHO KILLED RICHARD III

SUSAN FERN

AMBERLEY

Dedicated to Rob Gittins (scriptwriter for *Echo of the Dragon*, BBC Radio 4 1985), who thirty years ago encouraged me to write a book about Rhys ap Thomas – well, here it is!

First published 2014

Amberley Publishing
The Hill, Stroud
Gloucestershire, GL5 4EP

www.amberley-books.com

Copyright © Susan Fern, 2014

The right of Susan Fern to be identified as the Author of this work has been asserted in accordance with the Copyrights, Designs and Patents Act 1988.

All rights reserved. No part of this book may be reprinted or reproduced or utilised in any form or by any electronic, mechanical or other means, now known or hereafter invented, including photocopying and recording, or in any information storage or retrieval system, without the permission in writing from the Publishers.

British Library Cataloguing in Publication Data.
A catalogue record for this book is available from the British Library.

ISBN 978 1 4456 1980 4 (hardback)
ISBN 978 1 4456 1988 0 (ebook)

Typesetting and Origination by Amberley Publishing
Printed in Great Britain

Contents

A map of medieval Wales.

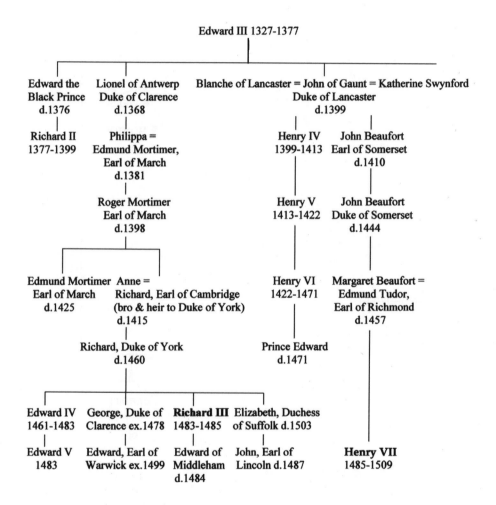

Edward III 1327-1377

Edward the Black Prince d.1376 — Richard II 1377-1399

Lionel of Antwerp Duke of Clarence d.1368 — Philippa = Edmund Mortimer, Earl of March d.1381 — Roger Mortimer Earl of March d.1398

Edmund Mortimer Earl of March d.1425

Anne = Richard, Earl of Cambridge (bro & heir to Duke of York) d.1415 — Richard, Duke of York d.1460

Blanche of Lancaster = John of Gaunt = Katherine Swynford Duke of Lancaster d.1399

Henry IV 1399-1413 — Henry V 1413-1422 — Henry VI 1422-1471 — Prince Edward d.1471

John Beaufort Earl of Somerset d.1410 — John Beaufort Duke of Somerset d.1444 — Margaret Beaufort = Edmund Tudor, Earl of Richmond d.1457

Edward IV 1461-1483 — Edward V 1483

George, Duke of Clarence ex.1478 — Edward, Earl of Warwick ex.1499

Richard III 1483-1485 — Edward of Middleham d.1484

Elizabeth, Duchess of Suffolk d.1503 — John, Earl of Lincoln d.1487

Henry VII 1485-1509

The lines of York, Lancaster and Tudor.

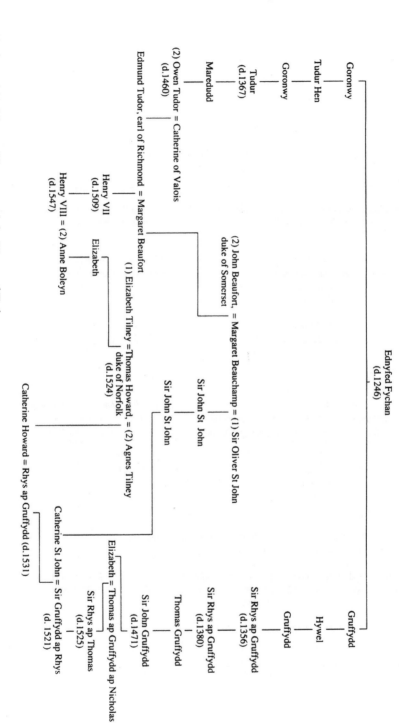

The line of Sir Rhys ap Thomas and the House of Tudor.

Introduction:
The Killing of a King

One of the most turbulent periods in English history took place between the years 1455 and 1485, and is known as the Wars of the Roses. The people of England and Wales were plunged into a series of bloody battles and conflicting loyalties that would end in the death of a king upon a field in Leicestershire. These dynastic civil wars were fought between the two branches of the royal house of Plantagenet, namely York and Lancaster, who both had legitimate claims to the crown. It all began when Henry Bolingbroke, the son of John of Gaunt, who was the third son of Edward III, deposed his cousin King Richard II in 1399. Henry became Henry IV, and his son Henry V was king for only a short while before his death in 1422, leaving behind a young heir, Henry VI. Henry VI was a weak monarch who suffered constant mental ailments and was unable to rule effectively in his own right. During his lapses in health, the Duke of York, who claimed descent from both the second and fourth sons of Edward III, was made Protector, but gradually the friction inherent within the nobility caused the duke to make a legitimate claim to the throne.[1] The first serious fighting between the houses of York and Lancaster commenced in 1455 at the First Battle of St Albans, where the duke was defeated.

The Duke of York then made his way to Ireland while his supporter Richard Neville, the Earl of Warwick, remained behind and managed to capture the king at the Battle of Northampton. The duke then returned to England and became Protector. However, there was still opposition from the Lancastrian faction, led mainly by Henry's wife, Margaret of Anjou. She led the Lancastrian forces north, where they clashed with those of the Yorkist faction at the Battle of Wakefield in 1460. The Duke of York and his second son Edmund were both killed, leaving his eldest son Edward, Earl of March, to continue the fight.

In 1461 Edward led his forces against the king at one of the bloodiest battles ever fought on English soil, at Towton in North Yorkshire. The battle lasted ten hours, and according to medieval accounts the losses were enormous: 10,000 Yorkists to 20,000 Lancastrians, which would have represented 1 per cent of the total population of Britain. Although this may be an exaggeration, there is no doubt that the loss of life was significant. Today there is little trace of the battle. No major tourist site marks the spot (unlike Bosworth). As one writer commented, 'Towton is consigned to the memory hole of oblivion from which it is only now being rescued by a few dedicated enthusiasts.'[2]

Edward achieved an overwhelming victory and was proclaimed Edward IV. However, this Yorkist revival would be short-lived. Edward fell out with his chief supporter, the Earl of Warwick, who then began to work tirelessly, at first to put Edward's brother, the Duke of Clarence, on the throne, then, when that proved unsuccessful, to reinstate Henry VI as king.

Edward spent two years trying to reclaim his throne, and in 1471 at the Battle of Barnet, Warwick was killed. Later, in May that year, at the Battle of Tewkesbury, Edward was once again victorious and Henry's heir, Edward, Prince of Wales, was killed. Finally unimpeded by any other claimants to the crown, Edward re-took the throne.

For twelve years England was finally at peace, but that ended abruptly in 1483 when Edward died unexpectedly, leaving behind a twelve-year-old boy, Edward V, as his heir – a recipe for disaster. Edward IV stipulated that he should be under the protectorship of his uncle Richard, then Duke of Gloucester, until he reached his majority. However, the young Edward's mother, Elizabeth Woodville, and her family had no liking for Richard, so they gathered together a faction of disaffected and ambitious nobles to thwart this plan. Desperate to maintain their former power and influence they seized the Royal Treasury and fleet, and tried to crown the young prince without Richard, planning to instate the queen's brother, Anthony Woodville, Earl Rivers, as Protector. However, Richard, aided by the Duke of Buckingham, apprehended the royal entourage at Northampton as it made its way to London. Anthony Woodville and others were arrested and taken to Pontefract Castle, where they were later executed without trial.

Richard and Buckingham then progressed to London, where the young prince was hailed as Edward V. However, events were to take a rather disturbing turn when Richard called a council meeting on 13 June, where he accused Lord Hastings of having conspired with the Woodvilles, using his mistress Jane Shore and Thomas Grey, Elizabeth's elder son, the 1st Marquis of Dorset, to act as go-betweens. Hastings was immediately executed, while the others were arrested and imprisoned. John Morton, Bishop of Ely, one of those who had also been arrested, was released into the custody of Buckingham.

The second, perhaps more significant, development was the revelation by clergyman Robert Stillington, the Bishop of Bath and Wells, that Edward IV's marriage to Elizabeth was null and void owing to an earlier contract Edward had made between himself and Lady Eleanor Talbot. This premarital contract rendered all his children by Elizabeth illegitimate.[3] The young Edward and his brother Richard were lodged in the Tower, from where they later disappeared. Their fate is still a topic of controversy.[4] On the 22 June a sermon was preached outside the old St Paul's Cathedral declaring Edward's children bastards and declaring Richard the lawful king. The nobles and commons of London met and drew up a petition imploring Richard to accept the crown. He accepted on 22 June and was crowned on 6 July as Richard III in Westminster Abbey.

Later in 1483 a conspiracy was hatched among a number of the disaffected gentry, many of whom were loyal to the memory of Edward IV. They planned to depose Richard and reinstall Edward V on the throne. In September, the leaders of the various conspiratorial factions made it known that Henry Stafford, the 2nd Duke of Buckingham, 'repenting of his past conduct, would rise to their support at the head of all his mighty forces'.[5] It was then that Buckingham revealed that the two princes had been put to death, but he refused to say who had done the deed. Naturally suspicion fell upon Richard, although it is not clear why he would have done so because their illegitimacy would have rendered them unable to legally take the throne.

Buckingham's defection and betrayal must have been a great blow to Richard, who had given him two vast grants of concentrated authority and patronage. He was first given power of supervision of all subjects in Shropshire, Herefordshire, Somerset, Wiltshire and Dorset, and made constable of the royal castles. In the second grant he was made Chief Justice and Chamberlain in both North and South Wales. Buckingham may have had aspirations to take the crown himself, but was dissuaded by Bishop Ely, who pointed out to him that another rival had a much better claim. This was good enough reason for Buckingham to begin making overtures to Henry Tudor, Earl of Richmond, then in exile in Brittany. He urged him to come and rescue England from the grip of the tyrant and proposed a marriage between him and the eldest daughter of Edward IV, Elizabeth of York, to seal the bargain.

Richard had been on a royal progress when news reached him at Lincoln of Buckingham's defection. He had no armed forces with him; however he set the wheels in motion to rendezvous with his army at Leicester on the 20 October. Meanwhile Buckingham began his march from his castle at Brecon, summoning what forces he could from Wales and the Marches, and headed for Hereford, only to be harried by the Vaughan family and Lord Stanley. The weather also played a significant role in the demoralisation of his forces, with gales and torrential rain hampering their progress. There had also been a great storm at sea and Henry Tudor's ships had been forced to return to Brittany. Buckingham realised that his rebellion now had little hope of success. Panicking, he disguised himself and headed for Shropshire.

Seven days later Richard entered Salisbury without having fought a single battle, and it was to here that Buckingham was brought after being handed over by the Sheriff of Shropshire. Richard refused to see him despite his pleas, and on 2 November Henry Stafford, 2nd Duke of Buckingham, was beheaded for treason.

The year 1484 began badly for Richard when in April his only son and heir, Edward of Middleham, died. This was followed later in the year by the death of his wife, Anne, from consumption. A king without an heir is on shaky ground. Richard had two choices: the young Earl of Warwick, the son of his brother, the Duke of Clarence; or the Earl of Lincoln, the son of his sister Anne and the Duke of Suffolk. Warwick was still a child of only ten years and somewhat retarded, so Richard chose Lincoln as his successor, making him the Lieutenant of Ireland, a position bestowed by the House of York on the heir apparent.

Henry Tudor's campaign had been unsuccessful owing to the weather; the support he obtained from Duke Francis was also lessening as Richard had extracted a treaty from the duke not to support him. Elizabeth Woodville was also urging her son, the Marquis of Dorset, who was with Henry in Brittany, to do likewise. Nevertheless, on Christmas Day Henry took an oath in the Cathedral of Rennes to marry Elizabeth of York and unite the houses of Lancaster and York. The gauntlet had been thrown down.

In the following year Henry Tudor began to fare slightly better. He had fled in exile to Flanders when he was warned of the treaty between Richard and Duke Francis. From here he managed to obtain permission from the French king for his English exiles to take refuge in France. Once he arrived on French soil he was able to muster support for his cause, aided by his uncle Jasper Tudor. He made overtures to the French nobility, and because it was expedient for them that the English could be put into turmoil with a possible civil uprising, he was soon supplied with troops, money and ships to enable him to make his bid for the English crown.

While Henry was making his preparations, rumour reached him that Richard intended to wed the young Elizabeth. This made Henry's objective even more urgent. It seems unlikely that Richard had any such intention, but rumour-mongering was rife at the time and this particular rumour certainly galvanised Henry into action. By the spring of 1485, Henry's fleet was rigging at Harfleur.

Richard's major problem was assessing exactly where this fleet would land. The south-east was one possibility, but there was no certainty of this, so Richard moved to Nottingham Castle with his army. Nottingham was fairly central so he would be only a short distance away from any of the possible landing sites, from here it would be quicker to intercept the invaders. However, the one place they gave little consideration to was Wales. Since the death of Buckingham, Wales had been controlled piecemeal by the principal chieftains in South Wales and the Stanleys in the North. Richard had shown favour to the Welsh and now counted on their support. Rhys ap Thomas, the principal chieftain of South Wales, declared for Richard, vowing that Henry Tudor would have to cross over his body to get into Wales. Not long after making this statement, Rhys declared to Henry that he would welcome him and offered him his support. Henry's uncle Jasper Tudor was Earl of Pembroke, and had already begun to make preparations for Henry's arrival, which included a great deal of propaganda designed to stir up Welsh national feeling. Henry was half Welsh by virtue of his father Edmund Tudor, and his followers claimed he was descended from a long line of Welsh kings. In fact they stated that he was the new 'Arthur'.

On 7 August Henry's fleet landed at Milford Haven on the tip of Pembrokeshire near the village of Dale. On landing, Henry fell to his knees and uttered the words *'Judica me Deus, et discerne causam meam'*, after which he kissed the ground and made the sign of the cross.[6] Henry had a force of 2,000 French mercenaries under the command of his uncle and the Earl of Oxford, but this would be no match for the forces of Richard, and he desperately needed to gather more recruits to his banner. The army reached Haverfordwest, 10 miles away, when Henry received news that both John Savage and Rhys ap Thomas had shifted their allegiance back to Richard. This was indeed a crushing blow.

They continued their march along the coast to Cardigan, where the small garrisons they encountered were quickly overcome or forced to submit. Some actually took up Henry's cause, swelling his troops, but many did not and he was still alarmingly undermanned. To the north-east, Rhys ap Thomas waited with his troops, but gave no indication which side he would join. In a desperate attempt to rally support, Henry offered Rhys the lieutenantship of all Wales if he would come to the aid of his fellow Welshman. It seems that this was a prize worth having, and so Rhys joined with Henry at Newton.

Marching under the dragon banner of Cadwallader, the bards proclaimed:

Jasper will breed for us a dragon –
Of the fortunate blood of Brutus is he
A Bull of Anglesey to achieve;
He is the hope of our race.[7]

Yet despite all the nationalistic fervour, few ordinary Welshmen flocked to the call, so Henry issued an ultimatum to those lords who had promised him support – the Stanleys, Lord Talbot and Henry's kinsman John ap Meredith – to join him immediately on pain of death. They replied that they were not ready to join, which must have made Henry feel very uneasy as his small force marched on toward Shrewsbury and away from the comparative safety of Wales.

On 11 August Richard received news of Henry's landing and by 19 August he was ready to leave Nottingham and make his way to intercept the advancing Tudor army at Leicester. Richard's forces numbered 9,000, while Henry's were 5,000. The two armies met at Market Bosworth in a battle that lasted only a couple of hours, with most of the actual combat possibly only lasting half that time.

The battle was decided when Richard made a charge toward the banner and person of Henry Tudor and may possibly have succeeded in striking him down, but for the last minute intervention of Lord Stanley, whose cavalry intervened to save Henry – the last act of betrayal for Richard. 'Treason' was the cry that echoed from Richard's lips on that day. The road to Bosworth ended with the death of Richard, 'fighting manfully in the thickest press of the enemy'.[8] His mutilated body was taken back to Leicester and subjected to many humiliations. The only epitaph for Richard came from the men who had known him

17

best. John Sponer rode to York to deliver news of his death to the townsfolk, 'that king Richard late mercifully reigning upon us, was … piteously slain and murdered, to the great heaviness of this city'.[9] Richard was the last King of England to fight in battle. Henry Tudor had secured the crown of England, and so began the foundation of one of the greatest of all English dynasties, the Tudors. This battle had been a pivotal moment in English history.

In 2013 a dramatic discovery in a car park in Leicester would reignite debate about this controversial period. The body of Richard III was discovered where it had been buried ignominiously at Grey Friars. This opened up exciting possibilities for historians. Was Richard the monster that he had been portrayed as for the last 500 years, or had it all been Tudor propaganda? The bones were subjected to rigorous modern scientific scrutiny. Yes, it was true that Richard had been deformed by a disease to the spine, but not enough to make him the hump-backed villain of Shakespeare's portrayal. Naturally, some questions remain. Did he murder the young Princes in the Tower? Was he truly a villain of grotesque proportions, murdering all who stood in the way of his ambitions? There are many historians who believe not, but sadly the bones cannot answer these questions.

Significantly, what the examinations did show was that the final death blow to Richard had been delivered by a halberd[10] to the back of the head. The chronicler Jean Molinet records that the blow was dealt by a Welshman,[11] and the contemporary Welsh poet Guto'r Glyn goes further and actually names the assassin.[12]

It appears the man responsible for dealing this death blow was the same man who had sworn fealty to his king only to betray him when offered a greater incentive – Rhys ap Thomas. Knighted on the field of battle by Henry, Rhys would rise to even greater prominence under the Tudor dynasty, becoming Lord of South Wales. However, his dynasty was to be short-lived when the family fell from grace during the reign of Henry's son, Henry VIII. Like Richard, Rhys also ended his journey with the Grey Friars, but in his home town, Carmarthen. He had taken himself there to die – an act of remorse, perhaps, or an echo of a betrayal long ago on a battlefield in Leicestershire?

This work is not intended to provide a thorough history of the Wars of the Roses, neither is it intended to provide a history of the reigns of the monarchs involved. There are many excellent, in-depth books on these subjects, which can be found in the bibliography. This is the story of one Welshman and the life and times in which he lived. A man who helped shape the course of English history with one fatal blow. Rhys ap Thomas, the man who killed Richard III.

1
Gruffydd ap Nicholas:
The Rise of the Raven
(1430–1474)

Wales played a distinctive role in the Wars of the Roses, not least because the ultimate victor, the first Tudor king, was part Welsh. Wales consisted of principality shires and Marcher lordships that were deeply affected by the wars, and, of course, the subsequent establishment of the Tudor dynasty. Unlike modern-day Wales, the principality did not encompass the whole of the country. It comprised a strip of land along the west coast secured by the great castles built by Edward I when he pacified the country at the end of the thirteenth century.[1] The castles of Harlech, Aberystwyth, Carmarthen, Caernarfon, Conway, Flint and a host of others all had small royal garrisons. Lying between the principality and the border with England were the Marches, over which Marcher lords held sway. They set taxes, and generally did as they pleased, paying little regard to the susceptibilities of the local population. Although the Welsh were looked upon as barbarous by the English overlords, many local Welsh gentry adopted English ways and customs and were highly educated men.

The administration of the principality was overseen by the Prince of Wales' council, comprising eight to fifteen members, which sat in London (later in Ludlow). This council acted as the final Court of Appeal for the principality. The lands were divided into two regions: those lands under direct royal control, and those lands that had been distributed by Edward I as feudal lands. The two territories under royal control were North Wales, whose headquarters were at Caernarfon, and South Wales, whose headquarters were at Carmarthen. The territories in these domains were organised into shire counties, of which Cardiganshire and Carmarthenshire were two; the headquarters of the latter were situated at Carmarthen Castle. These shire counties were administrated by a chamberlain, and under him were bailiffs, sheriffs and coroners who were responsible for collecting taxes and administering justice.

Following the rebellion by Owain Glyndŵr, the situation in Wales had rapidly deteriorated. While Henry V reigned, the government of the principality had been effective, but during the long minority of his son, Henry VI, this process of deterioration began. Henry VI's assumption of personal power in 1437 led to a massive misuse of royal patronage, with local offices (which local leaders regarded as theirs by right) being given to members of the royal household. The appointment of magnates as justiciars, for example, Humphrey of Gloucester (in North Wales in 1427 and South Wales in 1440) and the Earl of Suffolk (in South Wales in 1436 and North Wales in 1440) meant that there was a lack of supervision from the top. Local community leaders were virtually given free rein to do as they pleased, and added to this was the continued absence of many of the Marcher lords. Local men, like Gruffydd ap Nicholas, could now take advantage of the situation, and he virtually ran South Wales as if it were his own private lordship. As the historian

Carr remarks, men such as Gruffydd were 'a symptom, not the cause of the changing political situation'.[2]

During the Wars of the Roses many of the leading protagonists held lands and lordships in Wales, especially in the Marches. The years between 1450 and 1500 saw many of these shires and lordships change hands with alarming frequency. For example, the lordship of Glamorgan passed from the Beauchamp family to the Neville family to Richard of Gloucester (later Richard III) to Jasper Tudor in 1486 and finally in 1495 to his great-nephew, Henry, Duke of York (later Henry VIII). The six counties of the principality had been ruled by Henry VI; by his son, Edward of Lancaster, Prince of Wales from 1456; from 1461 by Edward IV; from 1472, Edward V; and from 1483 by Edward of Middleham (Richard III's son). They were eventually to be held by Henry Tudor.

The Wars of the Roses did not really affect many ordinary Welsh subjects, but the leading squires and landowners, for obvious reasons of self-preservation, gave their allegiance to their lords and so were brought into the conflicts. This, therefore, resulted in Welshmen fighting for both sides, for example, at the Battle of Mortimer's Cross in 1461, men from the south-west of Wales were fighting on the Lancastrian side, while those from the south-east were fighting for the Yorkist cause.

It was not only allegiances that prompted landowners to take sides; family feuds also played a significant role in determining which side they fought on. A good example is the Vaughans of Tretower who were under the lordship of Henry Stafford, Lord of Brecon. They adopted attitudes to Richard III and Henry Tudor that had as much to do with their kinship to the

Herberts of Raglan as with the bitter blood feud between them and Jasper Tudor. Tudor had executed Roger Vaughan at the Battle of Tewkesbury in 1471 simply because Vaughan had executed Owen Tudor at Mortimer's Cross ten years earlier.

In Wales, powerful local families were the backbone of society, however, they often exploited their situation while simultaneously trying to avoid any obligations. The lowlands and ports of the south were in communication with Ireland, the Low Countries and France, so there were plenty of opportunities for enterprising individuals to advance their position and standing within the community. The local gentry often chose contingents from their localities for service in foreign wars. This small number of indigenous families helped determine the course of the wars. Eventually, these men replaced the Welsh princes and absentee English magnates, and one family in particular, that of Gruffydd ap Nicholas,[3] seems to have played a unique role in the south of Wales in the century after 1430, and consequently in the establishment of the Tudor dynasty.

Gruffydd ap Nicholas's family traced their descent to Elidir Ddu, a Knight of the Holy Sepulchre and a Knight of Rhodes. His journey to the Holy Land may have been inspired by the Knights Hospitallers of St John who had a commandery at Slebech (Pembrokeshire). The ruins of the church still remain. However, later poets would trace the line back even further to Urien Rheged, the sixth-century legendary king of the northern British.[4] Rheged's crest was three black ravens, which the family were later to adopt as their own emblem.

It was Gruffydd ap Nicholas, the grandfather of Rhys ap Thomas, who began the family's rise to prominence. Legend has it that Gruffydd's father died on his wedding night from a wound, never seeing the son that he begot, a story similar to that of Henry Tudor, who likewise never knew his father. This may or may not be true, but it is clear that the early Welsh propagandists attempted to link the family with the Tudors in any way they could.[5]

In the aftermath of the rebellion by Owain Glyndŵr,[6] Gruffydd set about exploiting the political, social and economic opportunities in South West Wales during the decades prior to the outbreak of the Wars of the Roses. In 1415 he and his cousin Rhys ap Gwilym ap Phillip took up various administrative positions in the lordship of Kidwelly, and across the river Twyi in the county of Carmarthen. Carmarthen was the largest borough in Wales; the area was prosperous and consisted of small, scattered communities, large royal castles and small market towns. In 1424 Gruffydd was engaged by the Steward of Kidwelly, Sir John Scudamore, as his deputy, a position that gave him judicial authority in the lordship. The following year he surveyed the king's castle, demesne and boroughs of Dinefwr and Newton. In 1426 he became Sheriff of Carmarthen, a three-year term of office that gave him jurisdiction over properties that had been left without an heir and that would be transferred to the Crown. By the year 1429, Gruffydd was acting as deputy constable of Dinefwr Castle. All these positions gave him the opportunity to obtain property and wealth. By the mid-1430s Gruffydd was not only an important royal official in the lordship of Kidwelly and principality of Carmarthen, but was tenant of an expanding estate in the Twyi valley, which extended from as far south as Llanelli, and was also a burgess of Dinefwr and Dryslwyn.[7]

However, Gruffydd had a ruthless streak, and was always ready to exploit any opportunity that came his way. For example, he took advantage of his brother-in-law's being in France to eject him from the shrievalty[8] of Carmarthen and to occupy the position himself. Nevertheless, those in power found him to be a generally reliable officer. When Edmund Beaufort, a kinsman of the king, succeeded Scudamore as constable of Carmarthen Castle and Steward of Kidwelly in 1433, he continued to employ Gruffydd as his deputy steward. Indeed, Gruffydd moved in prominent circles. He married his first wife, Mabli, the daughter of Marreydd ap Henry Dwnn, of the notable Kidwelly family. His second wife came from an even more prestigious background; she was Margaret, the third daughter of Sir Thomas Perrot. By 1436/7 Gruffydd was in a position to achieve even greater ambitions in Wales, and to that end he sought formal letters of denizenship, which Parliament approved on the 2 March 1437.

In the counties of Cardiganshire and Carmarthenshire the king's justiciars and chamberlains were men of baronial rank who rarely visited the principality, therefore they relied heavily on their lieutenants. Men such as Gruffydd ap Nicholas and his sons enjoyed supreme political and administrative dominance in their area of South Wales (excluding parts of Pembrokeshire). Gruffydd held the position of chief justiciar, presiding over the petty sessions in Carmarthen and acting in the absence of Lord Audley. This was a position he held from 1444 to 1456; he also acted in place of Edmund Beaufort in Kidwelly. He was in a position that offered political, governmental and social control of the whole Twyi valley.

For an ambitious man like Gruffydd, the powers obtained also brought the temptation to carry out some less-than-noteworthy deeds. In 1446, Gruffydd's son John and his brother-in-law John Perrot secured by unsavoury means a sixty-year lease of the castle, towns and demesnes of Dinefwr, his ancestral home, for a rent of £5 per annum. In the years that followed, Gruffydd made his presence felt in Carmarthen. In October 1449, Gruffydd, Rede, and another influential burgess lawyer, Lewis ap Rhys Gethin, who was Mayor of Carmarthen, farmed the revenue of the entire town between them by drawing up a twenty-year lease of £20 per annum; as Griffiths says, 'a grant of considerable potential in the exploitation of Carmarthen's wealth to their collective profit'.⁹ Also, as time went by, Gruffydd had less to fear from other royal officers such as Edmund Beaufort, constable of Carmarthen Castle, and his patron; his cousin, Rhys ap Gwilym ap Phillip, who was well regarded by the absentee sheriff; the Earl of Ormond or indeed any of the local landowners. With Gruffydd's power base gradually extending – his sons now holding lieutenantships – he set his sights on the county of Cardiganshire, in the northern part of the principality of South Wales.

Between the years 1436 and 1441 there were a number of deaths in the Clement family, who held considerable estates in Pennard and Genau'r Glyn in the northern half of Cardiganshire. Gruffydd was responsible for determining who Phillip Clement could marry, and when Phillip died he was succeeded by his brother. Two-thirds of the family property was placed in the custody of Gruffydd and Edmund Beaufort; six years later they acquired another two-thirds, when William Clement died, leaving only a daughter as heiress. This was the prelude to a more concerted advance into Cardiganshire, one filled with violence and lawlessness.

This advance into Cardiganshire was led by Gruffydd's youngest son, Thomas ap Gruffydd, who was aided by two men from the lower Tiefi valley, Einion ap Jenkyn and Rhys ap Dafydd (whose father had served with Henry V in France), and Gruffydd ap Thomas, a leading official from the area. They were opposed by two landowners, but it seems that these landowners were outmanoeuvred and victory went to Thomas and his party. However, the landowners did not let it rest, for they lodged an appeal with the King's Council to secure the countermanding of Gruffydd's authority in South Wales.

In 1439 Gruffydd and his son Thomas, along with accomplices, were summoned to Westminster, but Gruffydd pleaded that he was too ill to come. However, he was not too ill to challenge the right of Westminster to summon such a case in view of the fact that Carmarthenshire and Cardiganshire had 'a Justice and Chamberlain and Chancery with full power for to try and determine all manor matters down there'.[10] As may be expected, the inquiry at Carmarthen later in the year was inconclusive, and it was postponed until the next meeting of the Great Sessions. However, Gruffydd had set his sights firmly upon Cardiganshire, and when John Dier, who held most of the estates there, died in September 1441, his heiress was conveniently found guilty of a felony, and so the lands were forfeit and leased by his lieutenants under his son Thomas.

To combat the lawlessness, other assertions of royal authority followed under Edmund Beaufort and Lord Audley; even Humphrey, Duke of Gloucester, held sessions at Carmarthen in 1442. According to the records many fines were imposed, but Gruffydd managed to avoid reprimands. It is also ironic that while Thomas was sheriff in Cardigan, many felons who had assisted Gruffydd and his sons to obtain the lands managed to escape from prison.

Gruffydd's other two sons also supported their father's ambitions. The eldest, John, leased Dinefwr with him in 1439, but after that records become unclear about his fate, and we hear no more of him. The second son, Owain, was very similar to his father in his ruthless ambition, and he carried on with Gruffydd's plans to control Pembrokeshire. It was clear that he had his father's support; as the poet Lewys Glyn Cothi writes:

> Gruffydd gives three ravens of the same hue;
> And a white lion to Owain,
> Many a young man under the sun
> Wears linen bearing these.[11]

Owain's ventures into Pembrokeshire were carried out with the same amount of lawlessness that Thomas had employed in Cardiganshire. The local people were terrified – one lady, Margaret, the pregnant widow of Sir Thomas Malefont of Upton, had placed herself under the protection of Glamorgan man Lewys Leyshon when she wished to make a journey to visit her mother in London. The irony is that she was abducted by this same man with an accomplice during her journey through the Gower.

Nevertheless, the activities of Owain and his band were causing grave concern to the government. In March 1443, when the Abbot of Whitland and Gruffydd were summoned before the King's Council to explain Owain's behaviour, Owain was ordered to be arrested the same day, but it appears that little was actually done – no doubt because of Gruffydd's control of the government of the principality.

Owain continued to rampage through Pembrokeshire, installing himself in the port of Tenby. By the early 1450s he was living in the town, even sitting on the courts alongside the bailiffs and the mayor. His following consisted of men from Carmarthenshire, who assisted him in robbing, assaulting and holding to ransom Pembrokeshire men. Every effort to have him arrested was ignored, and by July 1452 the government was so concerned about the inability of its local officials to do anything positive that they appointed the receiver of Pembroke to deal with the matter. This man was none other than Sir John Perrot, Owain's uncle, so it was hardly surprising when in September, Owain and the parson of Carew, Philip ap Rhys, received pardons for a whole range of offences, including armed uprisings.

Carmarthen was now the seat of power, presided over by Gruffydd. His ambitions and their achievement had gone from strength to strength. However, in 1447 he made a mistake which could have cost him dearly. He joined the retinue of Humphrey of Gloucester, who was then Justiciar of South Wales, on his journey to Bury St Edmunds. The journey ended in Humphrey's imprisonment and subsequent execution for treason in February of that year. When Humphrey was arrested, Gruffydd was hauled in front of the King's Bench, however, he was soon released and returned to his duties in South Wales.

Gruffydd soon appropriated the castle at Carmarthen with the idea of making this his permanent abode, and began converting it into a fortified residence. Its constable was his absent patron Edmund Beaufort, so it was easy for Gruffydd to use the financial resources of the Crown, which were at the disposal of the Chamberlain of South Wales, to complete the

refurbishments. In the years 1452 to 1453 he spent roughly £64, an enormous amount at that time.

In around 1451–3 Gruffydd presided over the 'eisteddfod' in Carmarthen. This was a competition for poets, and it increased his reputation in the contemporary literary circle of Wales. Poets lauded his achievements, lineage and influence. Lewis Glyn Cothi, a Carmarthen poet, called him 'the eagle of Carmarthen'; Gwilym ap Ieuan Hen lauded him for his learning and his talent as a judge, praising the fact that he had not been removed from office. Rhys Llwyd ap Rhys ap Rhiccert called him a second Alexander, the bearer of King Henry's standard. Gruffydd's sons had won him ascendancy in other parts of the principality; Thomas in Cardiganshire and Owain from Twyi to Tawe. He was especially honoured by the poet Dafydd Llwyd of Mathafarn, who perhaps went a little too far and hailed him as Carmarthen's Constantine the Great.

Lead the van, party of Urien,
We are waiting for leaders;
Raise your splendid and ancient banner,
Your ravens, and rout the Saxons;
Lead, man, in one course,
With the tamed ravens of the son of Urien of old.[12]

Gruffydd ap Nicholas was a remarkable man, nevertheless, his reign was coming to end when civil wars threatened to engulf the nation. He was 'a man of hot, fire and choleric spirit; one whose counsels were all in 'turbid, and therefore naturally fitly composed and framed for the times; very wise he was, and infinitely subtle and crafty, ambitious beyond measure, of busy, stirring brain'.[13]

The developments that had occurred in England during the fourteenth century no doubt played a significant role in allowing such men as Gruffydd to advance their own interests. The withdrawal of personal aristocratic lordship was a main feature, and one which was accentuated by the seizure of the English crown by the House of Lancaster. After the rebellion by Owain Glyndŵr it became obvious that to try and govern Wales according to Henry IVs penal laws would be well-nigh impossible. After 1415, Henry V and his brothers were occupied with the wars in France. In the years between 1420 and 1440, during the reign of the boy king Henry VI, aristocratic faction was rife, and when the king came of age the focus was centred on his household and court. Therefore, local power in Wales devolved on to local men, men such as Gruffydd, which resulted in the situation whereby the Crown became powerless to reassert its authority.

Gruffydd exploited English feudal and land law for his own interests in both town and countryside, leasing or mortgaging lordships, accumulating wardships, acquiring marriage settlements for his family and carefully placing his own sons in positions of power. However, Gruffydd displayed a great deal of devotion to Henry VI. He alerted the king on two occasions (1448 and 1450) to threats to the coast and shipping in South Wales, and swore his loyalty when news reached Wales of the arrival of the Duke of York from Ireland.

In 1453 the king's health gave cause for concern. Gruffydd's position became unstable as the country descended into civil war. Now the areas held by the magnates in South Wales became more significant. Gruffydd experienced difficulties with three of them – first the Duke of York, then Jasper Tudor and finally Humphrey Stafford, Duke of Buckingham – all of whom held Marcher lordships close to Gruffydd's base of operations.

In 1452 Jasper Tudor had been created Earl of Pembroke and the following year Gruffydd was ordered to hand over the lordships of Cilgerran, Emlyn Is Cuch and Dyffryn Breuan. In 1454 Richard, Duke of York, became Protector of the Realm, and the council over which he presided called Gruffydd and his sons, Thomas and Owain, to account for abusing their offices. They were reminded of Henry IV's law relating to Welshmen holding offices, and the council made it very clear to the absentee lords that these men should be removed. Gruffydd sought refuge with the Duke of Buckingham in Brecon, however he got into trouble with the Escheator of Hereford and was arrested, having fifty marks in his purse. He was later rescued by his son-in-law Sir John Scudamore.

Around the same time as this trouble in Hereford was occurring, the exchequer auditors called a halt to Gruffydd's expenditure on Carmarthen Castle, and the council also decided to review some of the judicial decisions he had made. Two associates of Gruffydd's had been placed in custody in Carmarthen Castle; now they were pardoned and offered safe conduct. They were then assaulted by men who were obviously in the pay of Gruffydd, and remained in the castle. Civil war was now plaguing the country. After the Battle of St Albans, in which the Duke of York was victorious, one of the men, Gruffydd ap Dafydd ap Thomas, again appealed to the Royal Council, claiming that Gruffydd had denounced him as one of York's servants and threatened him with even harsher treatment than before.

York had replaced Edmund Beaufort as constable of Carmarthen and Aberystwyth castles, and the Steward of

Kidwelly was now Edward, the son of York's brother-in-law. Gruffydd ap Dafydd ap Thomas complained once again, this time to Parliament, that the castles of Carmarthen, Cardigan, Aberystwyth, Kidwelly and Carreg Cennen were still in Gruffydd's hands. Gruffydd was ordered to vacate the fortresses straight away, otherwise he would suffer the most severe sanctions. He was ordered to bail himself to the sum of £3,000 for his good behaviour and his appearance before the king. In future, if anyone occupied the castles, they would be attained on a charge of high treason. A further blow to Gruffydd came with the Act of Resumption in 1456, which deprived him of his most special grant, the castle town and demesnes of Dinefwr, which were transferred on a twenty-year lease to Sir William Herbert of Raglan, one of York's retainers.

Not long afterwards he was faced with yet another challenge to his authority; this time it came from the Lancastrian camp. Jasper Tudor's elder brother Edmund, Earl of Richmond, was sent to South Wales to reassert the king's authority against the growing power of the Duke of York. Edmund was described as being 'at war greatly in Wales'[14] with Gruffydd, for Edmund Tudor had taken control of Carmarthen Castle and had probably established himself in Pembrokeshire in place of his brother Jasper. Two months later war broke out between Edmund Tudor and the Duke of York's retainers from the eastern Marches, led by Sir William Herbert and Sir Walter Devereux. Edmund was taken prisoner, and the castles of Carmarthen and Aberystwyth were transferred to York.

The year 1455 marked the beginning of the Wars of the Roses. Richard, Duke of York, who held important offices of state, had challenged Henry VI's right to the throne, and a series of bitter quarrels ensued between the council and other Lancastrians, especially the queen. Although there had been frequent skirmishes between the two rivals' supporters, these had never yet erupted into full-scale war; this time, however, they did. Richard, along with Richard Neville, the Earl of Warwick, defeated the Lancastrians under the command of the Duke of Somerset at the First Battle of St Albans. Peace finally prevailed, and the Duke of York was restored to full power and made Lord Lieutenant of Ireland by Henry. However, the Lancastrians, aided by Margaret of Anjou, Henry's queen, did all they could to undermine Richard's position. Violence erupted once again, and Richard was forced to flee to Ireland.

Gruffydd now had to decide which side he was on – the royalist Lancastrians or the House of York. At first he sided with Sir William Herbert, but in 1456 he came to an arrangement with Edmund Tudor whereby he and his sons received a full pardon for all their misdemeanours. By 1457, he was serving as Mayor of the Borough of Carmarthen. It seems Gruffydd made the right choice, for when Edmund Tudor died at Carmarthen in 1456, his brother Jasper took up the royalist cause, eventually triumphing in South Wales. In 1457, York surrendered the castles at Kidwelly, Aberystwyth, Carmarthen and Carreg Cennen to Jasper, in return for £40 per annum, and Jasper took up residence in Tenby, where he began to fortify the town (the town walls are still visible today).

Events were moving swiftly; in 1458 the Earl of Warwick, who held the port of Calais, began to attack vessels from Spain and Lubeck, both of which supplied the English court. Warwick was summoned to London to answer for his actions, but this resulted in both Warwick and York refusing to answer the summons and thereby being indicted for rebellion. Warwick invaded England and captured Henry; York returned and became Protector of England. However, the queen and other prominent Lancastrian nobles assembled an army in the north of England. York had gone to Ludlow, but he still sent messages to Henry swearing his loyalty. His overtures, however, were ignored, so he set about fortifying his position. The Yorkists were outnumbered two to one, and the king, dressed in full armour, led his army against them. Just outside the town, at Ludford Bridge, the royal army bore down on the Yorkists – many of the Calais contingents refused to fight against the king and defected. With their troops severely depleted, the Yorkists had no option other than to flee. York went to Ireland with his second son, Edmund. The elder son, Edward, Earl of March, fled with Warwick and Salisbury to Calais.

The Yorkist leaders now planned an invasion of England, and Warwick joined Richard in Ireland to plan their strategy. At the end of June, Edward, Warwick and Salisbury landed at Sandwich (Kent) and marched on London. The Lancastrians had headed to Northampton with the king, and here Warwick caught up with them and captured Henry, who was brought to London and lodged in the Bishop's Palace. A popular ballad of the time sums up the general feeling: 'Send home, most gracious Lord Jesus most benign, / Send home thy true blood unto his proper vein, Richard, Duke of York...'

York set out from Ireland to claim the throne, but the lords would not countenance this; instead they declared that Henry was to have the crown for life, to be succeeded by York and his heirs, meanwhile York was to exercise the government as Protector. The queen was still at large, having initially fled with her son, the young Prince Edward, to Wales. After the battle at Northampton she had fled to Cheshire and had begun to gather an army of loyal northern lords. York rode out to intercept them, and although he was heavily outnumbered, he charged the main Lancastrian force just outside Wakefield. Here he fell, fighting valiantly. His second son, Edmund, escaped, but got only as far as the bridge, where he was captured and stabbed to death. The heads of York, Edmund and Salisbury were sent to decorate the chief towns of Yorkshire, with the Duke of York's head being sent to York, where it was stuck on Micklegate and capped with a crown of paper and straw.

The events of the next few months saw the fighting escalate rapidly, but by then Gruffydd was an old man, and it is very likely that he died soon after the events at Wakefield. Records are unclear as to exactly what his fate was. The claim in the *Life of Sir Rhys ap Thomas*, that he was killed at the Battle of Mortimer's Cross in 1461 fighting alongside Edward, Earl of March (later Edward IV), seems highly spurious, and was designed, no doubt, to earn him a place on the winning side. For two decades he had been unrivalled in South Wales, enjoying a dominance that was matched only by the later deeds of his grandson, Rhys ap Thomas.

One of his last acts was to make the castle and lordship of Narberth and the lordship of Efelffre, which he had acquired from York, over to his son Owain in February 1460. When he died, his body was taken to the Grey Friars in Carmarthen, where it was accorded a place of honour before the image of St Francis. Both the body and tomb disappeared during the Dissolution of the Monasteries.

In February 1461, a major battle of the civil wars took place at Mortimer's Cross in Herefordshire. The Lancastrian forces were led by nobles loyal to King Henry VI, his queen Margaret of Anjou, and their seven-year-old son Edward, Prince of Wales. The armies of York were led by the seventeen-year-old Edward, Earl of March, the eldest son of Richard, Duke of York, who had died at the Battle of Wakefield the previous year. The Welsh forces consisted of a large contingent from Carmarthenshire led by Jasper Tudor and his father Owen, who were fighting on the Lancastrian side, Owen having been the second husband of Catherine of Valois, Henry VI's mother. Among the Welsh forces were the two sons of Gruffydd ap Nicholas, Owain and Thomas.

It appeared that the battle was going in the Lancastrians' favour, but a disastrous move by Owen Tudor on the Yorkist left wing saw his army routed, and the day went to York. Owen fled toward Hereford, where he was captured and beheaded in the market place, 'his head was set upon the highest "grice" [step] of the market cross; and a mad woman combed his hair and washed away the blood off his face, and she got candles and set about him burning, more than a hundred'.[15] Jasper Tudor managed to escape. Edward and the Earl of Warwick entered London one month later, where he was proclaimed Edward IV.

During the battle a strange celestial phenomenon occurred, known as a 'parhelion', when three suns were seen to rise. The troops thought it a bad omen, but Edward, Earl of March, persuaded them that it was a sign from God in the form of the Holy Trinity and that God was on their side. He was later to adopt this as his emblem: the 'sun in splendour'. However, although the sun was shining on the House of York, these decades would be dark ones for the sons and grandson of Gruffydd ap Nicholas.

Quickly seizing the advantage, Edward rode north with Warwick in pursuit of the Lancastrian queen. At Towton, by far the bloodiest battle of the civil wars, the Lancastrians were completely routed, forcing the queen, her son and husband to flee to Scotland. For the next eight years an uneasy peace reigned, and Yorkist rule established itself throughout the country, with profound effects in Wales.

There are only fragmentary records for the family of Gruffydd ap Nicholas during this time, and the same is true for the principality as a whole. Royal administration in Kidwelly, Carmarthenshire and Cardiganshire was mainly sustained by locally appointed officers. What available records there are show that in Cardiganshire, rents were not paid, and courts were often suspended and records destroyed. The government of the principality and Kidwelly was placed in the hands of Yorkists such as Sir William Herbert and John Dwnn, who was given the constableship of Aberystwyth and Carmarthen castles for life.

The sons of Gruffydd appear to have been quietly eclipsed; the eldest Rhys may have already died, since there is no reference to him after 1450. Owain lived in a substantial house opposite Carreg Cennen Castle and was married to the daughter of the Pembrokeshire squire Henry Malefont. Thomas, the youngest, lived at Newton, in the house built by his father, and through his marriage to Elizabeth Gruffydd he obtained the lordship of Llansadwrn and built Abermarlais.

In the months that followed the battle at Mortimer's Cross, resistance to the Yorkist regime centred on these two brothers, and especially the sons of Thomas. In September 1461, Sir William Herbert was commanded to pacify the region. He took oaths of loyalty from Cardiganshire and Carmarthenshire, which brought in 1,400 marks to mark Edward IVs coronation. He went further by expelling the rebels from the king's castles, and Carmarthen's fortress was repaired.

Carreg Cennen was much more difficult, and here the brothers held out; it required a 200-strong force from Raglan commanded by Sir Richard Herbert and Sir Roger Vaughan to negotiate its submission. By May 1462 Owain and Thomas had surrendered; a garrison of eighteen soldiers was installed, and a large workforce of 500 engineers and labourers began dismantling the castle's fortifications over the next three months. Carreg Cennen was never to be occupied again.

The government wished to deny the brothers a focus for resistance, but this was no easy task to accomplish. The local population was divided in its loyalties, the execution of justice was disorganised, and revenue collection often disrupted. In 1464 an uprising took place at Dryslwyn about which we know very little. One of the ringleaders was Phillip Mansel from Oxwich in Gower, who was married to Mary, the brothers' sister, and who had been with them at Mortimer's Cross. The uprising may have been part of the feud that existed between Gruffydd ap Nicholas and Henry ap Gwilym of Cwrt Henri, located nearby. It is on record that both Thomas ap Gruffydd and Henry both farmed the castle and borough of Dryslwyn.

It may well have been this uprising that persuaded Thomas to escape into exile, along with many other Lancastrians, to Burgundy, taking with him one of his younger sons, Rhys. His elder sons, Morgan and Henry, continued to harass the Yorkists; there are many references to Morgan sweeping the enemy from west Pembrokeshire with North and South Wales 'rallying behind his ravens', and this may well be a reflection of Sir William Herbert's tightening grip on South and West Wales during the 1460s. In 1468 Herbert captured the last Lancastrian stronghold, Harlech. The ringleaders of the rebellion were offered a general pardon by Edward IV as an inducement to surrender. Morgan, Owain and Henry were excluded and singled out as renegade ringleaders.

In 1469 there was another outbreak of discontent. Warwick and his circle had been constantly passed over for various offices of state and honours, supplanted by the Woodville family. More importantly, however, the king and Warwick disagreed about foreign policy. Warwick and the king's disaffected brother, George, Duke of Clarence, fermented risings in the North. In July, at Edgecote, near Banbury, they defeated Edward's supporters and held the king prisoner. Seemingly, it was Warwick's intention to replace Edward with George on the throne. However, Edward gained the upper hand, and Warwick and Clarence were forced to flee to France, where they allied themselves with the King Louis XI and their former enemy, Margaret of Anjou.

When Herbert died at the Battle of Edgecote in 1469, Morgan and Henry seized Carmarthen and Cardigan castles. Edward IV sent his younger brother Richard, Duke of Gloucester, to recover them, and he was also authorised to offer a pardon, such was the force that the brothers commanded. In 1470 a commission was issued for South Wales, headed by Gloucester, who had now been appointed justiciar and chamberlain during the minority of the young Earl of Pembroke, William Herbert II. A meeting of the Great Sessions was held in Carmarthen, and the poet Lewis Glyn Cothi records that the Duke of Gloucester, accompanied by another young duke (quite possibly Henry Stafford, Duke of Buckingham), encountered four of Thomas's sons at Glasfryn – Morgan, Henry, Dafydd and Hopkin – together with other of their kinsmen. Gloucester represented the highest level of Yorkist authority, but the meeting probably achieved little other than to elicit an oath from them to prevent any further uprisings.

The following year (1470), Warwick and Clarence returned and deposed Edward, reinstating Henry to the throne; Edward fled to the Netherlands. The Readeption of Henry VI (1470–1)[16] was good news for Thomas's sons; they finally received a full pardon from Henry VI on 23 March 1471. This spell of rule was short-lived; Edward returned and outmanoeuvred Warwick. He regained Clarence's loyalty and decisively defeated Warwick at Barnet. Queen Margaret also retuned in the hope of aiding Warwick; when her ships landed at Sandwich (Kent), she heard news of Warwick's defeat and promptly headed west, hoping to reach Wales. Edward intercepted her and her army at the River Severn at Tewkesbury, where, on the 4 May, the penultimate battle of the wars took place. The Lancastrians were defeated and the young Prince Edward slain. Finally, the deposed King Henry was murdered in Tower of London, and Edward could now rest securely on his throne.

With the collapse of the Lancastrian regime, the sons of Thomas ap Gruffydd were offered a full pardon for all their offences. Morgan, an opportunist like his grandfather, saw the necessity to change sides, and obeyed Edward IVs commission to lay siege to Jasper Tudor and his nephew Henry in Pembroke Castle. After an eight-day siege, Dafydd assisted Jasper and

Henry in their escape to Tenby, and consequently to the port, so they could flee to France. 'The Earle departed from thence to Pembroke, whom incontinent Morgan Thomas, sent by King Edward, besieged, and kept in with ditches and trenches that he might not escape; but the viii th day following he was delivered from that distress by David, brother to the said Morgan, his assured faithful friend, and departed forthwith to a town by the sea side called Tenby...'[17]

Dafydd was the only brother to stay loyal to the Lancastrians.

It was about this time that Thomas and his son Rhys returned from Burgundy, although the records are unclear about the reason they came back to Wales. It was not long before Thomas fell afoul of the justiciar chamberlain William Herbert II, the new Earl of Pembroke. Pembroke visited West Wales in 1471 and 1474, accompanied by Sir Anthony Woodville, Earl Rivers, the Prince of Wales's chief counsellor, and he visited Carmarthen and Cardigan for the Great Sessions. It was during this visit that an encounter took place between Pembroke's men and those of Thomas ap Gruffydd. In a skirmish at Pennal, Thomas was killed. There are several accounts of how he died. One of the earliest writers says that the Earl of Pembroke seized his house at Abermarlais and goaded Thomas into retaliating from his hideout in Harlech; he died before the earl could track him down, and was buried secretly. Another writer adds that the burial took place among the saints on Bardsey Island.[18]

The History of the Gwydir Family, written by Sir John Wynn (1580–1616), also records the death of Thomas ap Gruffydd at Pennal, south of Harlech, just across the river from Cardiganshire. In this work it is suggested that the encounter was part of the ongoing feud between Thomas and Henry ap Gwilym of Cwrt Henri: 'Some affirm John ap Meydeth to have been at field in Penyal for Tho' Gruffith, which field was fought between Thomas Gruffith ap Nicolas and Henri ap Gwilim; and the earl of Pembroke's captains where Thomas ap Gruffith got the field, but received there his death's wound.'[19]

According to another work, *The Life of Sir Rhys ap Thomas*, Thomas ap Gruffydd was mortally wounded by Dafydd Goch, whom he killed. Goch appears to have been a Yorkist servant who had been rewarded by Edward IV with Stapleton in in the lordship of Maelienydd. Thomas, who was badly wounded, was finally despatched by a servant. In a poem written shortly afterwards by Dafydd Llwyd, who lived nearby, he said that Thomas died on Good Friday.

The exact date of the encounter is not known but it is likely to have taken place sometime between 1472 and 1474. The escheator of Carmarthenshire had custody of Thomas's property in 1473–4, before it was passed to his heirs, indicating that Thomas died sometime in 1473–4, although it is not clear how quickly the shire government would have acted.[20]

If this was not bad enough, the family also had quite a few personal tragedies to contend with, for, not long after Thomas's death, his sons Morgan and Dafydd also died, both without heirs. Of all of Thomas ap Gruffydd's legitimate sons, only Rhys seems to have been capable of heading the family. However, the position of the family had been neutralised while Yorkist rule had been imposed on Carmarthenshire and Cardiganshire. It would be in 1483, when the Duke of

Buckingham received extraordinary powers throughout Wales, including the custody of all the royal castles, that Rhys ap Thomas, Gruffydd's grandson, would be in a position to restore the family to prominence.

2
Rhys ap Thomas:
The Man Who Killed Richard III
(1474–1485)

The information that we have concerning the life of Rhys ap Thomas can be found in the seventeenth-century work aptly entitled *The Life of Sir Rhys ap Thomas* (later referred to as *Life*).[1] In keeping with all eulogies to great men, the work informs us that when Rhys was born in 1449, his father consulted his horoscope with regard to his future prospects. When he learnt that his son was to grow to be a man of high position and achievements he immediately set about finding the best tutors for him. It is possible that this story may be true, for Thomas ap Gruffydd had in his employ Lewis Caerleon, a scholar, who was later to become physician and servant to the queen, Elizabeth Woodville.[2]

In 1464/5, at the age of sixteen, Rhys went with his father to Burgundy, along with many other Lancastrian exiles, for reasons that are not entirely clear, to the opulent court of Philip the Good. At an impressionable age Rhys was exposed to court life, and not just any court, but one that was renowned throughout Europe as having one of the most civilised and progressive atmospheres for learning and chivalry. The ducal lands of Burgundy spanned a geographical area of 500 miles

from north to south. There was a 30-mile gap that separated
the north and south that was always under threat from the King
of France. Although the dukes of Burgundy held no royal titles,
they took measures to make the lands they held from the French
king more independent, and they tried to develop a sense of
loyalty among the nobility by allowing them to take one third
of the aides levied from their tenants. The duke could not rule
alone so he needed the support of the nobility especially, as well
as other groups of subjects. Philip the Good became a great
patron of the arts and crafts, and his library was one of the
finest in Europe. In all respects the court of Burgundy outshone
those of France and England.

Another important aspect that helped Philip secure an
identity among the nobles was the institution of the Order
of the Knights of the Golden Fleece. This was chivalric order
that implemented a code of conduct for knights. It emphasised
courage in battle, loyalty to one's lord, protection of the weak
and the defence of Christianity. Rhys would be exposed to all
these influences in the nine years he spent here, and we can gain
some insight into his participation in court life from the *Life*.

> One time Duke Philip taking a view of his army, he fortuned to
> find young Rhys at the manage, and observing the gracefulness of
> his riding, the comeliness of his person and the settled soberness
> of his behaviour, he sends for Thomas ap Griffith, the father,
> whom he had long known and had ever highly favoured, both for
> his courtesy and courageous carriage, on all occasions; making
> it an earnest suite unto him to have this young gentleman, his
> son, for his servant, which the father yielded to …
>
> *Life*

And so the duke placed him with the Earl of Charloys, who

> presented him a pubic horse and admits him unto pay, following
> him in his own ways from which his lordship saw no reason to
> disagree. And now young Rhys begins to show what metal he
> was made of and that to be in continual action was his chief
> delight; for he was ever either practising of arms or playing at
> his weapons, running wrestling riding swimming, walking and
> under-going all those military duties imposed upon him with
> cheerfulness and alacrity ... thus continued this young spark
> running in a fair even course, til, passing through all inferior
> offices, he was now climbed up that step as gave him title of
> captain ...
>
> *Life*

Having received the best military training as well as the best
tutorship, Rhys returned to Wales with his father in 1474, a
young man equipped with much knowledge and military
expertise that would stand him in good stead for the times
ahead.

During the 1470s the fortunes of the sons and grandsons of
Gruffydd had gradually been eclipsed by the ever-increasing
presence of Yorkist administration. When Rhys returned
sometime after 1474 there was a very different system
operating in Wales, which gave the family little room to regain
their previous position. In 1472 the two-year-old Prince of
Wales was formally granted the revenues of the principality,
which included Carmarthenshire and Cardiganshire. Political
circumstances over the following four years saw the Prince's
Council grow in number and become entrusted with more

extensive powers of governmental oversight. The structure of the principality remained the same, but the council did intend to make control of the area more effective.

The council now had its base at Ludlow, but many councillors and administrators, some of high rank, regularly visited Cardigan and Carmarthen to hold meetings of the Great Sessions and, more importantly, to demonstrate the power of regal authority. Among these high-ranking officials were Anthony Woodville, the prince's uncle and senior counsellor; Hugh Huntley, an experienced administrator, especially in the duchy of Lancaster's Welsh lordships, who presided over the Cardigan and Carmarthen sessions; and John Herbert, a kinsman of the 2nd Earl of Pembroke. Administrators loyal to the House of York acted on the earl's behalf as deputy chamberlains of South Wales due to the earl's minority.

Apart from Huntley and Herbert, there were other loyal York men in charge of affairs. Richard Mynors, an usher of the king's chamber; Sir John Dwnn, who was steward of Kidwelly and Carmarthen castles; and John Morgan of Tredegar, who was acting as chamberlain in the years 1473–5. The Earl of Pembroke might hold the title of Justiciar-Chamberlain and Steward of Cantref Mawr and Cardiganshire, but it was the Prince's Council that directed affairs, and its authority extended to a number of the Pembrokeshire lordships.

In 1479 this was dominance was intensified, due in part to the dispute between the Vaughans and the Herberts that had divided Pembrokeshire since 1473/4, enabling rebels to seize Pembroke Castle in 1478. Further riots in the east and at Aberystwyth Castle were also indicative of the instability of the region. In 1479 the earl and Sir William Herbert were forbidden to cross into Wales over the River Severn for a year. This was the prelude to the earl's removal as Justiciar and Chamberlain of South Wales. His earldom was exchanged for that of Huntingdon. Elizabeth Woodville managed to persuade her husband to pardon all the contestants in 1479, in fact, many efforts had been made to end the disputes between prominent Yorkists and bring reconciliation to Pembroke. In the same year, an effort was made to commend the new regime to the locals of Carmarthenshire and Cardiganshire by offering, for the first time, to pay officers of the commotes an annual fee.

The county of Pembroke was transferred to the prince 'for the reformation of the well public, restful governance and ministration of justice in the said parties of south Wales'.[3]

A few months earlier, Huntley had replaced the Earl of Pembroke as Justiciar of South Wales, Steward of Cantref Mawr and had also taken over the lordship of Llanstephan. Mynors was appointed Chamberlain of South Wales and Steward of Cardiganshire the following day. For the next four years they governed the principality shires, aided occasionally by others of the prince's commissioners. These men included the Bishop of St David's, Robert Tully, Sir William Young of Shropshire (he was also Steward of Haverford from 1479 and Pembroke from 1480), Thomas Limericke and John Twyneone (two Gloucestershire lawyers), and John ap Rhys (the prince's attorney general in all his lordships and counties of South Wales).

This reorganisation of government in South Wales meant that Gruffydd's family played no part in the running of their home territory during the 1470s and early 1480s. The actions of the justiciars, chamberlains and constables of the castles of Carmarthen, Cardigan and Aberystwyth were rarely in the hands of local men. At Dinefwr, the place that had special significance for Gruffydd's family, John Herbert (one of the Vaughan family) was in charge during the mid-1470s. For the remainder of the period, Henry ap Gwilym's brother, Lewis, and their nephew Morgan were farming the borough, castle and demesnes at Dinefwr. This replacement of Thomas ap Gruffydd by Henry ap Gwilym was the source of the ongoing feud between the two families that had resulted in Thomas's death. Indeed, the family of Gruffydd ap Nicholas had every right to feel resentful of their treatment.

In 1473, when Thomas was killed and his elder brothers had died, Rhys became his sole heir. His brother Dafydd had only one daughter, therefore Rhys inherited all the family fortunes. The *Life* tells us that Rhys surrounded himself with wise counsellors. Among them was John, Bishop of St David's and a learned priest; Robert, Abbot of Talley, who was a Lancastrian sympathiser and had been removed from the see by Edward IV; and John, Prior of Carmarthen. He also counted among his counsellors Morgan of Kidwelly, who was 'skilled and qualified' in the laws of England; Richard Griffith and Arnold Butler, two very experienced captains; and Robin of the Dale, an astrologer who Rhys frequently consulted.

Having surrounded himself with these wise counsellors, during the next ten years of Yorkist rule Rhys began to rebuild his family's reputation and standing within Wales. The first matter to be dealt with was the long-standing feud between his family and that of Henri Gwilym of Cwrt Henri, a feud that had resulted in his father's untimely death. A marriage between Rhys and Eva, the co-heiress of Cwrt Henri, was arranged to help cement new bonds of kinship, which both parties agreed to and which brought Rhys a fortune as well as more loyal supporters. With this marriage and the new alliances it brought, Rhys now decided to put his house in order and take care of his family.

The *Life* says that he was renowned for holding an open house, 'that the gentry did continually flock there as to some academy, for their civil nurture and education, by which means his house was so frequented, and he so well attended, that whenever he came in respect of the greatness of his train, he bare show rather of a prince than a private subject.' (*Life*)

He also was a patron of poets; many of them gravitated to his houses at Abermarlais, Carmarthen, Newton and especially Carew. These included poets such as Guto'r Glyn (1435–93), who, though mostly active in north-east Wales, visited Abermarlais, and Tudur Aled (d. 1525), one of the most esteemed of all Welsh poets. He died while visiting Rhys in 1525 and was interred in the Grey Friars church in Carmarthen. In later years Rhys patronised many others literary persons as well as theatre troupes.

The years spent at the Burgundian court had served Rhys well, allowing him to impress his fellow Welshmen to such a degree that he soon began to gain their confidence, and more importantly their allegiance. Holding such courts was a costly business, but Rhys was frugal when it came to his own expenses and kept well within his yearly revenues. He dressed modestly except when he had to attend official events. The *Life* describes him as 'homily in his appearance'. He kept only a few servants and was modest in his diet, and this comely behaviour was another attribute that gained him favour among his peers.

His greatest challenge, however, was to turn his people away from the rough, unruly manner in which they had become accustomed to living, and instil civility and good order. *Life* states that he achieved this through 'religion and conversation'. Rhys employed the Bishop of St David's to instigate a survey of all the churches in the diocese. Religion had fallen by the wayside during the tumultuous period of the wars, and many clergy had abandoned their churches. Rhys set about finding the funds to reinstate them to their former glory and to employ incumbents to take charge of them. He also instituted festival days, on which sports and dances could take place, even on occasion joining in with the merrymaking. Places of meeting were appointed and summerhouses erected. No doubt this was a reflection of the courtly procedures that he had become accustomed to while in Burgundy, but they had the desired effect and resulted in more civilised behaviour from his countrymen.

The political situation in England was still far from secure, and Rhys bore in mind the possibility of further strife. He employed two captains, Richard Griffith and Arnold Butler, to train young gentlemen and others who were deemed worthy for military discipline. They were to receive daily exercises in the art of warfare, which at first was not well received, but once they saw the benefits of such training, many others flocked to enlist. The *Life* also tells us that he found a way to endear all his countrymen by

Turning all such lands as he had in demesnes, into horse races, as that of Carew, Narberth, Emyln, Abermarlais, Weobley or other of his great houses, and as they increased he would bestow on this man or that a horse, by which means drawing in those of the best abilities in all the adjacent counties, he tied them strongly to their former proffers, so that now with the help of his tenants (which I find upon record to be between eighteen and nineteen hundred, and all of them bound by their leases to be ready with a horse when he called upon them) ... For as he gave them horses they gave him certain patches of land within their estates.

Life

By these devices Rhys was able to summon between 4,000 and 5,000 men at very short notice. It appears that Edward IV was happy for Rhys to continue in this manner and viewed him as a loyal subject, for Rhys gave no indication that he was seeking any personal advancement. So great was his popularity that the bards sang, 'All the Kingdom is the Kings, / Save where Rice does spread his wings.'[4] Rhys, however, was not amused, and made the bard Lewis Glyn Cothi change the words to 'The Kingdom is the King's, / The skirts of France and Rice is his.'

Rhys had been farsighted in his actions because the tide of events was soon about to turn once again. On 9 April 1483, Edward IV died suddenly, leaving as his heir the twelve-year-old Prince Edward. On his deathbed Edward made his brother, Richard of Gloucester, Protector of the Realm. Richard rode out with Buckingham to meet the young prince at Northampton to escort him to London for his coronation. The prince was travelling with his uncle and guardian, Lord Rivers. They did not wait at Northampton for Richard, but headed to Stony Stratford, where they spent the night. Rivers arrived at the inn where Richard and Buckingham were staying and explained why the royal entourage had moved on, Stony Stratford being that much closer to London. Fearing a plot to oust him from his position as Protector, Richard kept Rivers prisoner at the inn and rode at first light to escort young Edward to London. Accompanying the prince were his half-brother Lord Richard Grey, and Sir Thomas Vaughan, both of whom were arrested.

Richard and Buckingham then escorted a rather bewildered and frightened young prince into London to await his coronation. The queen and her eldest son, the Marquis of Dorset, decided that the boy should be wrenched from Richard's grasp, but this idea gained little support from the nobles, so they fled, taking with them the treasure from the Tower. The queen took sanctuary in Westminster Abbey with her daughters and younger son Richard, Duke of York, Prince Edward's brother.

The prince finally entered London on 4 May. Lord Rivers was sent to Sheriff Hutton, Grey to Middleham Castle and Vaughan to Pontefract to await their fate. Edward's coronation was postponed until the business of the protectorship had been established and a government formed. The young prince was installed in the state apartments of the Tower and a date was set for his coronation, 24 June. However, the Woodville family still posed a problem, for the queen refused to leave sanctuary and was gathering a disaffected group of nobles to her cause, including Lord Hastings and Bishop Morton.

There were more surprises in store when Robert Stillington, Bishop of Bath and Wells, revealed to Richard that Edward's children were bastards, owing to the fact that the late King Edward had already been pre-contracted to marry Eleanor Talbot. Such contracts were binding and once entered into meant that that the persons concerned were married in law, therefore Edward's marriage to Elizabeth Woodville was null and void. This was a blow for Richard, who could see that if the children were illegitimate then his protectorship was on shaky ground, especially as the Woodville conspiracy against him was gaining strength.

On 10 June he acted, appealing to the North for military aid against the Woodvilles and calling on the Earl of Northumberland to take command of the expedition. He addressed the mayor, alderman and commons of the city of York:

We greet you well, and as you love the weal of us, and the weal and surety of your own selves, we heartily pray you to come unto us to London in all diligence you can possible after the sight hereof, with as many as ye can defensibly arrayed there to aid and assist us against the Queen, her blood adherents, and affinity, which have intended, and daily doth intend, to murder and utterly destroy us and our cousin the Duke of Buckingham, and the old royal blood of this realm, as it is now openly known, by their subtle and damnable ways forecasted the same, and also the final destruction and disinheriting of you and all other inheritors and men of honour, as well of the north parts as other countries, that belong to us; as our trusty servant, this bearer shall more at large show you, to whom we pray you give credence, and as ever we may do for you in time coming fail not, but haste you to us hither'.[5]

Before the messages arrived in York, Richard had taken action against Hastings and the Woodvilles. On 12 June he appointed two meetings of councillors for the following morning. One group, headed by Chancellor Russell, was to discuss certain matters at Westminster relating to the coronation. The second group was requested to attend the council chamber in the Tower at 10 a.m. It consisted of Hastings, Stanley, Rotherham, Morton, Buckingham and Howard. Richard began the proceedings by informing them of the conspiracy that he had uncovered; he accused Hastings, Stanley, Morton and Rotherham of plotting against him. They denied this, but it was too late, with cries of treason the door flew open and armed men entered and arrested them. Morton and Rotherham were escorted to the Tower, Stanley was put under house arrest and Hastings was dragged out for execution on the green by Tower chapel. Bishop Morton was placed in the custody of Buckingham, who removed him to his castle at Brecon.

Richard now took steps to deal with the Woodvilles. On 16 June, accompanied by armed men, they surrounded the sanctuary where the queen had taken refuge. The Archbishop of Canterbury and Lord Howard went to plead with the queen to release the Duke of York so that he may attend his brother's coronation. Finally, much against her wishes, she surrendered the boy, who joined his brother in the Tower. Now Richard took the decision that Rivers, Vaughan and Grey would have to be executed. On 24 June, Rivers and Grey were brought to Pontefract Castle – Vaughan was already there – and on the next day they were beheaded.

It was now that the council, having learned of Stillington's revelation concerning the illegitimacy of Edward's children, urged Richard, as the sole heir, to claim the crown. On 22 June, Richard and Buckingham, accompanied by a train of magnates, rode to St Paul's Cross to hear Friar Shaa commend Richard as the true king. The Lords and Commons gave their approval and the coronation date was set for 6 July. Two weeks later the king and his wife, Anne Neville, set out on progress throughout the kingdom. They were gone just a little over eight weeks when the first rebellion of Richard's reign broke out, and from a most unexpected quarter.

In May 1483 the Duke of Buckingham had received extraordinary powers in Wales. He was given custody of all royal castles and unlimited powers to appoint local officials. The following week he received authority to 'supervise all our subjects'[6] and to array them armed whenever the king had need of them. There was now no opportunity for Rhys or any of his kinsmen to recover the family's former position. This state of affairs was not to last for very long, for six months later Buckingham rebelled against Richard.

The precise details of how and why he did so are rather obscure. The most comprehensive, yet sometimes unreliable source for this episode of the medieval period is the *Croyland Chronicle*. According to this work, the rebellion had begun in the southern and south-western counties, with the aim of restoring Edward V to the throne. This was followed by two other conspiracies that had slightly different motives. By the end of September 1483, three separate conspiracies were amalgamating into one concerted effort to remove Richard from the throne. Suddenly it appeared that Buckingham, up to now a loyal supporter and beneficiary of Richard, had made it known that he was joining the uprising: 'repenting of his past conduct, [he] would rise to their support at the head of his mighty forces'.[7] Furthermore he dropped the bombshell that the Princes in the Tower had been murdered, but by whom it was not clear.

The *Chronicle* states that the purpose of Buckingham's rebellion was to place Henry Tudor on the throne, aided by his then prisoner John Morton, Bishop of Ely. At Morton's suggestion a messenger was sent to Margaret Beaufort, the mother of Henry Tudor, who despatched her man Reginald Bray to Brecon. If Buckingham had harboured hopes that he could take the crown then no doubt Morton put him straight. Henry Tudor had a better claim to the throne and was unmarried, so he was free to marry the eldest daughter of Edward, the Princess Elizabeth; this would be a panacea to the Woodville faction. If Buckingham was successful then he too could play the 'Kingmaker', as Warwick had done previously. Buckingham assembled his tenants and retainers; all the bailiffs and stewards of his Welsh lands had been charged that at their master's call they must bring to the field every man they could find.

Rhys ap Thomas did not join in the rebellion. The reason that is given is because of the animosity between the duke and Rhys's family. The *Life* explains as follows:

There was a deadly quarrel between the Duke of Buckingham and Rhys ap Thomas and both blown to so high a pitch of defiance, as that the duke some days before had sent him a cartel, threatening him withal, in a lofty and arrogant language, to come and cudgel him out of his castle in Carmarthen if so be that some speedy satisfaction were not given his lordship for injuries received that Rhys ap Thomas in manner stout enough though somewhat better seasoned with courtesy made answer that the ways being mountainous and craggy, his grace might spare the labour, for that he intended in person shortly to attend his lordship at Brecon…

It appears that a Doctor Lewis, one time tutor of Rhys's, was the intermediary between them and managed to effect a reconciliation, which took place at Trecastle, midway between Brecon and Abermarlais. However, this was to little avail, as Rhys decided not to join with the duke and instead played the waiting game.

The date was set for 18 October when simultaneous uprisings would begin from Maidstone to Exeter. The men of Kent and Surrey were to seize, or at least to threaten, London. The men of Devon and Dorset were to march eastward. Henry Tudor, with a strong contingent of men supplied by the Duke of Burgundy, would land on the South Coast. Buckingham would advance south-eastward, crossing the Severn. Meanwhile Richard had been on progress through the country and did not learn of Buckingham's betrayal until 11 October.

Within hours of receiving the news Richard had issued his first commands to the council at Westminster, and planned to rendezvous with his army at Leicester on 20/21 October. Three days later he launched his campaign by leading his army to Coventry. However, he had not been marching long before he had news of Buckingham's ill luck. Since 18 October Buckingham had been moving east from Brecon, but had been harried by a force under the command of the Vaughans, who effectively cut his communications with Wales while at the same time raiding the lands of Brecon Castle. The weather had been particularly foul, which had also hindered progress. Finally the duke reached Herefordshire, but he only had his own retainers and those Welshman that could be threatened or coerced into joining him; by the time he reached Weobley his army was disintegrating.

Morton made his escape to Ely and later to Flanders; Buckingham realised he had been duped by Morton and so in panic he put on rough clothing and galloped northward to Shropshire to seek a hiding place. On 28 October Richard entered Salisbury without having fought a skirmish. A few days later Buckingham was brought as a captive to the city. He had sought shelter with a servant of his, Ralph Bannester, who had turned him over to the sheriff of Shropshire, who conveyed him to Salisbury. He was tried, found guilty of treason and was executed on 2 November.

Henry Tudor's venture had also failed. Duke Francis had provided him with fifteen ships and 5,000 Breton soldiers and they had sailed from Paimpol on 31 October. On the first night the fleet had been scattered by storms and most of the vessels had been driven back to Normandy or Brittany. The next day Henry arrived just off the coast of Dorset with only two ships; he saw that the coast was lined with troops. He sailed to Plymouth, where he learned of Richard's victory over the rebels, so he promptly headed back to Nantes, where he received a loan of 10,000 crowns from Duke Francis to help him and his flock of exiles.

For the time being Richard was free from threat, for within two weeks of setting out from Leicester the king had disposed of a great rebellion. The rebellion had failed, mainly because of apathy on the part of the nobles; not a single baron or earl had joined the cause against Richard. No town of any consequence had been won over, and those who had sprung to arms had been quick to desert.

At Christmas in 1483, while the king held court at Middleham across the channel in Brittany, another ceremony was taking place in the cathedral at Rennes. Henry Tudor took a sacred oath to marry Elizabeth, the daughter of Edward IV, and unite the red and white roses. His followers knelt and paid him homage as though he was already king.

With the sudden demise of Buckingham, Richard had improvised a piecemeal supervision of the Welsh Marches. Richard Huddleston was made constable of the castles of Beaumaris and Anglesey, and captain of the towns. Thomas Tunstall became constable of Conway, and also gained many other, lesser, positions. Sir William Herbert took the Chief Justiceship of South Wales. It would appear that Richard now sought to attract local men of importance. In February 1484 he gave out lesser rewards for good service, over half of them to Welshmen, and among them was Rhys ap Thomas, to whom he granted an annuity of 400 marks for life. This was the first indication of Yorkist favour to any member of the family since 1465.

1484 was a disastrous year for Richard, although he did manage to come to terms with his bitterest rival, Elizabeth Woodville. On 1 March in an assembly of lords he took the following oath:

I Richard ... promise and swear, *verbo regio,* that if the daughters of Elizabeth Grey, late calling herself Queen of England ... will come to me out of the Sanctuary of Westminster, and will be guided, ruled, and deemed after me, then I shall see that they be in surety of their lives and also not suffer any manner of hurt ... nor them nor any of them imprison ... ; but I shall put them into honest places of good names and fame honestly and courteously shall see to be founden [supported] and entreated [treated] and to have all things requisite and necessary for their exhibitions and findings as my kinswomen; and that I shall do marry [arrange for the marriage of] ... them to gentlemen born, and every of them given in marriage lands and tenements to the yearly value of 200 marks for term of their lives ... And such gentlemen as shall help to marry with them I shall straightly charge lovingly to love to entreat them, as wives and my kinswomen, as they will avoid and eschew my displeasure.

And over all this I shall yearly ... pay ... for the exhibition and finding of the said Dame Elizabeth Grey during her natural life ... to John Nesfield one of the esquires of my body, for his finding to attend upon her the sum of 700 marks ... ; and moreover I promise to them that if any surmise or evil report to be made to me of them by any person ... that then I shall not give thereunto faith nor credence, nor therefore put them to in any manner punishment, before that they or any of them so accused may be at their lawful defence and answer ... [8]

The *Croyland Chronicle* says that only the daughters came out of sanctuary; there is no mention of the queen doing the same. She must have believed Richard's promise for she sent messages to her son, the Marquis of Dorset, who was in Brittany, urging him to abandon Henry Tudor, which he readily did – only to be captured by Henry Tudor's men when he reached Compiegne and was 'persuaded' to return.

Richard, fearing the possibility of invasion, now moved his headquarters to Nottingham Castle at the heart of his kingdom. However, tragedy struck, for in the middle of April he received news that his young son Prince Edward had died. This was a major blow for Richard, both personally and dynastically; every king needs an heir, otherwise his position is seriously jeopardised. There were two possible candidates; the son of his brother Clarence, the ten-year-old Earl of Warwick, who was retarded, or the son of his sister Anne and the Duke of Suffolk, the Earl of Lincoln.

It was not until 21 August that Richard decided to create Lincoln Lord Lieutenant of Ireland, a position that was associated with the House of York's heir. The *Croyland Chronicle* also tells us that Richard took all necessary precautions for the defence of his party against the exiles in Brittany. He established a system of posts whereby a messenger could be despatched 200 miles within two days, and to keep an eye on Henry Tudor he sent agents into Brittany, from whom he could learn his enemy's movements.

The next few months were full of problems, for while Richard was preparing for the invasion from Brittany he had also been forced to find the means to combat the threat from the Breton fleet, the Scots fleet and French corsairs. He also had to find men of war to take action against English pirates that were causing trouble, which he eventually managed to contain. By midwinter Queen Anne was gravely ill, most probably suffering from tuberculosis. The year ended with the Yeomen of the Crown riding in all directions bearing martial commissions, proclamations against the rebels and warnings to coastal towns to ready their defences against invasion.

In March 1485 Anne died. She was no sooner buried than rumours began to circulate concerning Richard and his niece Elizabeth. It was alleged that he planned to marry her, something that seems extremely unlikely considering she had been bastardised, which would then have rendered Richard a usurper. If he wanted to deny her to Henry Tudor he could have easily married her to some other gentleman. He promptly issued a denial:

It is so that divers seditious and evil disposed persons enforce themselves daily to sow seed of noise and disclaudre against our person and many of the lords and estates of our land, to abuse the multitude of our subjects and aver their minds from us ... some by setting up of bills, some by messages and setting forth of lies some by bold and presumptuous open speech and communication one with another, where through the innocent people would live in rest and peace, and truly under our obeisance ... be greatly abused and oft time put in dangers of their lives, lands and goods, as oft as they follow the devices of the said seditious persons, too our great heaviness and pity ...[9]

Meanwhile Henry Tudor had heard news of Richard's intention and was 'pinched by the very stomach'. He sought to make other arrangements for a substitute bride, then he learnt of Richard's denial. He could not afford to waste any more time and began in earnest to make plans to invade. Since he had been in France he had had a difficult time – he had been suing various lords and councillors for aid, in fact he had been required to go 'a begging' – and by the spring all his efforts had borne fruit. He knew he had to act soon, for Dorset's defection had shown that he might not be able to rely on his followers in England or his band of exiles. He finally extracted a promise from the King of France of money, troops and ships. He was given a force of 2,000 men, however, these were not regular troops, but prisoners from the Normandy gaols, promised freedom if they helped Tudor's cause. Henry left the Marquis of Dorset and John Bouchie in Paris as pledges for the 40,000 livres that the government of King Charles had advanced.

Richard learned that Henry's fleet was rigging at Harfleur, but there was no indication of whereabouts in England they would land. Richard despatched Sir George Neville to sea with a fleet to watch the channel and guard the harbours of Kent. Viscount Lovell was sent to strengthen the coastal defences and muster the forces of the southern counties. The Duke of Norfolk remained in East Anglia to guard the approaches to London. Invasion was imminent, but when and where could not be ascertained. What was abundantly clear was that both sides needed all the support they could muster.

According to later writers, Trahaearn ap Morgan, a lawyer of Kidwelly, advised Henry to make his landing in Wales, where he would be assured of support. These plans were, however, jeopardised early in May when John Savage was arrested in Pembroke, where he had been intriguing on Henry's behalf.

On 21 June Richard issued another proclamation against Henry Tudor:

Piers Bishop of Exeter, Jasper Tidder [Tudor] son of Owen Tidder calling himself Earl of Pembroke, John, late Earl of Oxford and Sir John Widville with other … rebels and traitors [who] have chosen to be their captain one Henry Tidder, which of his insatiable covetousness … usurpeth upon the name and title of royal estate of this realm.[10]

By now Henry Tudor had become a key figure in the opposition to the king, and along with other prominent Welshman he also tried to gain Rhys's support for the Lancastrian cause. Trahaearn ap Morgan was employed by those involved with Henry Tudor's interests to persuade Rhys, via Doctor Williams.

Morgan of Kidwelly a discreet man and a close friend to the said Rhys to whom he [Doctor Williams] delivered the true state of the business, and how far all things were advanced in England for the common good, imploring him for God's cause, whose honour was highly abused by Richard's unjust usurpation, for his country's sake, for his own safety, and the preservation of all good men who were joint sufferers in these grievous calamities, to employ all his wit and industry to imprint in Rhys a true feeling of so pious, just and honourable undertaking, so that he might deliver up the keys of that part of the kingdom (now in his custody) to the assured pledge of our weal, the renowned Earl of Richmond …

Life

Finally he sent word to France that Rhys and John Savage were willing to support another insurrection against King Richard, but how reliable this information is can be questioned. It appears that Rhys was ambivalent in his choice of sides and did not declare straightaway his support for Henry Tudor. As Griffiths remarks, the projected invasion was similar to other ventures during the past thirty years when Rhys's family were urged to support one side or another in the English dynastic quarrels. On the other hand, the circumstances of the years 1484–5 had offered an opportunity for the family to repair its depressed fortunes and recover the social and political dominance it had enjoyed in West Wales.[11]

On 1 August 1485 Henry's fleet set sail for Britain, the day of reckoning for Richard was fast approaching.

3

The Road to Bosworth

In a characteristic precaution during the later months of 1484, Richard required Rhys to take an oath of fidelity to the king and to hand over his only legitimate son, Gruffydd ap Rhys, as a hostage. Rhys responded to the king by a letter, written from Carmarthen by the Abbot of Talley. It read as follows:

I have received letters mandatory from your Majesty, wherein I am enjoined to use my best endeavours for the conservation of your royal authority in these parts to apply likewise my soundest forces for the safeguarding of Milford Haven from all foreign invasion; especially to impeach and stop the passage of the Earl of Richmond, if so by any treacherous means he should attempt our coasts; and withal Sir, an oath of allegiance has been tendered me in your Majesty's name by certain commissioners, deputed (as it seems) for that fidelity. Touching the first Sir, now an enemy is declared, I hold myself obliged without looking any further into the cause, faithfully to observe the same, by a necessary relation, my obedience, hath to your Majesty's commands, to which I deem it not unseasonable to annexe this voluntary protestation; that whoever ill affected to the state, shall dare to land in those parts of Wales, where I have any employments under your Majesty, must resolve with himself to make his entrance and irruption over my belly. As for my oath Sir, in observance to your Majesty's will, I shall ever regulate mine. I have, (though with some heart's grief I confess and with reluctantly of spirit), as was required, taken the same before your Majesty's commissioners, and if stronger trial than either faith or other might be laid upon me to confirm my most loyal affection, I should make no delay to *emannacle* and fetter myself in the strictest obligations for your Majesty's better assurance.

And here I beseech your Majesty give me leave without offence to disburden myself of certain cogitations, whereby I am persuaded, that these pressings of vows and oaths upon subjects, no way held in suspect, have often times wrought even those of soundest affections, a sensibility of some injury done to their faith; a thing which heretofore has been prejudicial to many great princes, who, while they showed themselves distrustful, and feared subtle dealing, have read to some of fickle minds and unstable thoughts evil lessons against themselves. I speak not this Sir as repining at what I have done; but to give your Majesty, to witt, that I fear some evil offices have been done me, which might you think yourself unsure of my service without this manner of proceeding. Whatever, Sir, other men reckon of me, this is my religion, that no vow can lay stronger obligation upon me in any matter of performance, than my conscience. My conscience binds me to love and serve my King and country my vow can do no more. He that makes shipwreck of the one, will (I believe) make little account of the other. For my own part Sir, I am resolutely bent, while I am to spin out my days in well doing; and so God willing to conclude the last actions of my life. And sure Sir could

I find myself culpable of one single cogitation, repugnant to the allegiance I owe your Majesty, I should think that life I have lived overlong. Now Sir for the delivering of my son to your Majesty's commissioners as a gauge of my fealty, I have as yet presumed on this short pause, not in way of opposition to your commands, but to fit myself with such reasons, as shall I hope in no sort seem discordant with your will. The years, Sir, that my poor child bears on his back are but few, scarce exceeding the number of four, which I conceived, might well privilege him, being more fit for the present to be embosomed in a mother's care, then exposed to the world, nature as yet not having the leisure to initiate him in the first lecture of feeding himself. Again, Sir, be pleased to consider he is the only prop and support of my house now in being; and therefore may justly challenge at my hands a more tender regard then I can anyway expect he shall find among strangers, and in a place so far remote from his natural parents. And lastly, Sir, I may well call him the one half of myself, nay to speak more truly the better part of me, so that if your Majesty should deprive me of this comfort, I were then divided in my strength, which united might perhaps serve as most useful were I called to some weighty employments for the good of your service. I humbly beseech your Majesty to reflect upon these necessities with an impartial eye, and in the meanwhile to be fully assured, that without these hard injunctions, I really am and will, how badly so ever I be entreated still continue,

Sir, your most humble,
Most obedient,
And most faithful
Subject and Servant
Rhys ap Thomas. From Carmarthen Castle 1484.[1]

There appears to be no further move by Richard to extract Rhys's son as a hostage, perhaps he understood all too readily the loss of an only son and he really had no reasons to doubt Rhys's loyalty. However, Richard now had more pressing issues; the weather had been good and Henry Tudor's fleet had managed to sail around Richard's fleet in the south-eastern ports unhindered. On the afternoon of 7 August Henry's fleet entered the bay at Milford Haven at the tip of Pembrokeshire. Just before sunset they landed on the north shore of the bay near the village of Dale. Henry fell to his knees and offered up a prayer: '*Judica me Deus et discerne causam meam...*'[2] He kissed the ground and made the sign of the cross.

The next day he marched 10 miles to Haverfordwest, where he received news from a delegation that had arrived from Pembroke: 'The inhabitants of Pembroke at the same very time comforted all their dismayed minds, for they gave intelligence, by Arnold Butler, a valiant man, demanding forgiveness of their former offences, that they were ready to serve Jasper their earl.'

Henry Tudor marched under the dragon banner of Cadwallader. The bards were singing about the coming again of Arthur:

Jasper will breed for us a dragon –
Of the fortunate blood of Brutus is he
A Bull of Anglesey to achieve;
He is the hope of our race.[3]

Yet despite such a rousing call to arms, Henry heard that, ignoring their earlier oaths, both John Savage and Rhys ap

Thomas were now armed and ready to serve Richard's cause. It is possible that Rhys may have decided that caution was paramount and did not wish to reveal his allegiance – for he had much to fear from the long arm of Richard. Griffiths has suggested that he may have already declared for Henry and had been in touch with him when he landed. He says that Rhys may have employed this strategy deliberately to deceive and confuse Richard.[4]

Henry sent scouts on ahead as he cautiously marched toward Cardigan. They had gone barely 5 miles when rumour reached him that Sir Walter Herbert, the younger brother of the Earl of Huntingdon, was 30 miles east at Carmarthen with a 'great host', and was ready to intercept his army. Panic ensued, but fortunately for Henry this turned out to be a false report and the road to Cardigan was clear. More encouragingly, Richard ap Gruffydd ap John of Gower, a man of high parentage, arrived later at Henry's camp with some of his men, which helped to swell the ranks. Gower had been with Sir Walter Herbert and Rhys ap Thomas. Later the same day they were joined by John Morgan of Tredegar, also perhaps from Herbert and Rhys's army a little further east. Rhys was friendly with Morgan and Griffith and it is quite possible that this was a means by which Rhys could keep in contact with Henry without arousing suspicion.

The garrisons they came upon on the march were quickly overcome or persuaded to surrender. Nearing Cardigan, he learned that Rhys's forces were somewhere to the north-east, but Rhys was still giving no indication as to which side he would chose to fight on. Rhys needed to be cautious; if, as Griffiths suggests, he was already inclined to support Henry, then no one could know until the last minute in case word reached Richard. Griffiths says that between them Rhys and Henry may have devised the plan to distract Richard. Nevertheless, Henry must have always feared betrayal, and likewise Rhys must have been equally unsure of discovery; both he and Savage had much to fear from Richard's agents Sir James Tyrell and Richard Williams.

Rhys continued to shadow Henry and his army, if that is what it could be called, as it made its progress through Wales. A major disappointment for Henry was the fact that the people of Wales had not flocked to his banner and there had been no risings in support of their 'prince'. He would therefore be vastly outnumbered by Richard's forces unless Rhys would join him. Henry despatched riders with secret messages to those whom he considered his friends and supporters, outlining the route he would take: 'to pass over Severn, and through Shropshire to go to London, and therefore desired them to meet him, with whom in place and time convenient he would impart more of his intent.'[5]

Having despatched the messengers – Christopher Urswick to his mother Lady Margaret Beaufort, the Stanleys and Sir Gilbert Talbot, and another messenger to Rhys and Walter Herbert – he set off for Shrewsbury. The routes that Rhys and Henry followed independently toward Shrewsbury were not done randomly and must have been coordinated; Rhys marched up the Twyi valley to Llandovery, then east to Brecon, then north to Welshpool. Finally, Rhys had a meeting with Henry. Traditionally the place is said to have been Long Mountain, the high ridge overlooking Welshpool from the east. There, both forces are said to have spent the night of 16 August.

According to Polydore Vergil the outcome was not in doubt: '... whom Richard Thomas [Rhys ap Thomas] met by the way [toward Shrewsbury] with a great band of soldiers, and with assured promise of loyalty yielded himself to his protection'.[6]

According to the *Life* the meeting had been preceded two days earlier by one or more contacts between Henry and Rhys, presumably when Henry was between Machynlleth and Welshpool. Vergil confirms this statement: 'Two days before Henry had promised to Richard Thomas [Rhys] the perpetual Lieutenantship of Wales, so that he would come under his obedience, which afterward when he had obtained the kingdom he gave liberally.'[7]

The biggest uncertainty for Henry was the Stanley faction. The further he moved away from Wales toward the Severn valley, the greater the insecurity. When he had arrived at Shrewsbury on 12 August he had been received by the townsfolk and given promises from the Stanleys. Sir William was camped a few miles to the north-east and Lord Stanley lay a few miles east of the town. Stanley explained that his son was Richard's hostage so he could not show his hand, but he advised Henry to make toward Richard and not toward London. Realising they had little option, they advanced toward Newport, where Sir Gilbert Talbot brought Henry a contingent of 400–500 men.

Marching slowly, they reached Stafford, where he met with Sir William Stanley. The Stanleys, however, were still not fully committed; William Stanley promised to join Henry as soon as he had raised more troops, but it was apparent to Henry that they might not commit themselves until they saw which way the battle was going. Henry headed directly toward Richard at Nottingham, which had been sensible advice, for if they had advanced on London and were defeated, there would have been no hope of a safe retreat to Wales. The advance from Shrewsbury to Stafford pointed directly toward to Nottingham, but Henry may have felt that he was approaching Richard at too rapid a pace and of course he still needed reinforcements, so he veered south-east 17 miles to Lichfield.

On 11 August, when Henry had already reached Shrewsbury, news finally reached Richard of Henry's landing at Milford Haven. Richard immediately sent word to Lovell, Norfolk, Brackenbury and various other captains telling them to assemble their troops and meet him at Leicester. He also sent orders to Lord Stanley to come immediately to Nottingham. Stanley replied that he could not come because he had the sweating sickness, but he also managed to send word to his son Lord Strange, who was Richard's hostage, telling him to make his escape from Nottingham. Lord Strange attempted an escape only to be caught and interrogated – he revealed that his father and John Savage planned to desert Richard. He begged to be allowed to send his father a letter and pleaded with him to change his mind about supporting Henry and instead come to the aid of the king. Meanwhile, sheriffs of the realm were ordered to proclaim Stanley and Savage public traitors. It was at this time that Richard learnt of other betrayals, including that by Rhys ap Thomas.

On 19 August Richard left Nottingham and headed toward Leicester, taking with him Lord Strange, who had still not received a reply from his father. The Duke of Norfolk and men from the south Midlands were gathering at Leicester. William and Thomas Stanley were approaching from the west, behind them Henry's army; toward Richard's rear were the mounted forces of the Earl of Northumberland, ostensibly supporting Richard. Richard's army was indeed by far the larger, but everything depended on Stanley and Northumberland to whom they finally gave their allegiance. Just before sunset Richard crossed the north bridge over the River Soar and entered Leicester, dismounting at the White Boar inn, where he was greeted by John Howard. Northumberland sent word that he would be arriving the following evening.

That same evening Henry's army had left Lichfield for Tamworth, but Henry stayed behind with a small bodyguard, possibly to have some time alone with his thoughts. However, when he finally set out he got lost and could find no trace of his army, and as it grew dark he was forced to seek shelter in a hut some 3 miles from Tamworth. His uncle Jasper and the rest of his men became concerned, but there was little they could do until morning, by which time Henry appeared. On his arrival he was given news that Stanley wished to hold a conference with him at Atherstone, so he set off immediately with a small guard. Vergil recounts what happened there:

> Here Henry did meet with Thomas and William [Stanley] where taking one another by the hand, and yielding mutual salutation, each man was glad for the good estate of the others, and all their minds were moved to great joy. After that they entered in council in what sort to arraign battle with King Richard ... whom they heard to be not far off.[8]

Yet Henry must still have been aware that the Stanleys could not be relied upon. Lord Stanley kept remarking on the danger his son was in, and neither brother fully committed their forces at the outset. It was clear that although they wished to overthrow Richard, they would not join Henry until they were certain of his success. Henry knew his army could not afford to falter.

Richard meanwhile was supervising, along with Howard and his son, the Earl of Surrey, the mustering of his forces. Men were arriving in a constant stream and they needed quarters and positions allocated in the ranks. By late afternoon Richard learned from his scouts that Lord Stanley's army was at Stoke Golding, about 10 miles west of Leicester. His brother William had halted close by at Shenton, while Henry's army were about 9 miles to the rear. By evening Northumberland arrived at Leicester with his weary troops and horses.

On 21 August the royal army formed columns and marched through Leicester to the sound of drums along the road to Kirby Mallory, which lies between Atherstone and Leicester. Men-at-arms and archers of Norfolk, protected by a cavalry screen, provided the vanguard. Next in line came Richard, with Norfolk and Northumberland, at the head of knights, squires and chief officers of his household. The rest of the company was made up of men from the Midlands and the North. Behind the division followed the baggage train, and next from Leicester after the van was on its way was the rear guard, Northumberland's troops.

Richard rode on a white courser, he was cased in armour and had a golden crown on his helmet, and above him flew the banners of St George and England. When the army reached Kirkby Mallory, Richard halted to allow his men to eat and for him to confer with his commanders. He learned that the Stanleys still remained where they were and that Henry Tudor was beginning to move down Watling Street from Atherstone.

Richard and his commanders decided the best tactic was to take up a position that would allow them to monitor Stanley's forces, blocking the approach of the invaders if they were marching to give battle, or acting as a springboard to come down on their flank if they dared to follow Watling Street to London.

About 5 miles west of Kirkby Mallory the vanguard entered the village of Sutton Cheney, which stands on the eastern side of a high ridge that extends westward for about a mile. To the north the land slopes upward to the town of Market Bosworth some 2 miles away. Norfolk's vanguard came down from the ridge on to a stretch of land known as Redmore Plain. Richard led his troops past Norfolk to bring them on to higher ground at Harper's Hill; now the army, although separated, could be turned west or south to block any advance on Watling Street or Redmore Plain.

Henry's army turned off Watling Street and advanced toward Redmore Plain, and by evening they had left the road and were making camp. Henry's vanguard, fronted by archers, was commanded by the Earl of Oxford; the right wing was under the command of Sir Gilbert Talbot and Sir John Savage had the left. Henry governed the battalion, having with him his uncle Jasper, Earl of Pembroke, and Rhys ap Thomas with his cavalry.

On the night of 21 August, the armies were clustered around the dominant feature of the landscape, Ambien Hill, which rises to almost 400 feet and stands in the centre of the region. From part of the southern slope a marsh extends for about 50 acres. Richard had decided to use this location, but there were problems with his plan. For a start he lacked sufficient numbers of troops to hold the hill and provide Norfolk with the extra men he needed to extend his line across the plain. He could not rely on Northumberland to his right, and it might mean that Sir William Stanley could cross the ridge unopposed. However, after discussions with his captains, Richard decided to occupy Ambien Hill early in the morning. It was indeed a commanding position, and the flanks protected them from the Stanleys, but the main reason was that it afforded Richard the best chance of getting to Henry Tudor.

The following morning Richard addressed his men. He told them that whoever won the battle it would be the destruction of the England they knew. If Henry Tudor won he would crush all the supporters of the House of York and rule by fear. If he (Richard) won he would be equally ruthless and govern by force. One of his squires pointed out that there were no chaplains in the camp, to which Richard replied that was what he had intended. If their quarrel was God's then they needed no supplications, if not such prayers were idle blasphemy.

Norfolk sent word that he was ready to march. Richard despatched one last message to Lord Stanley telling him to come immediately if he valued his son's life. Then Richard's division streamed northward down the slope of Harper's Hill; ahead of them Norfolk's troops were ascending the rise into Sutton Cheney. On a tumulus north of the village Richard halted and sent a detachment of mounted archers and men-at-arms to proceed along the ridge to the crest of Ambien Hill. Richard received word from Stanley telling him that 'he had other sons and he was not in a mind to join the King'. Richard promptly ordered Lord Strange's execution, but at the last minute relented and had him put under close guard instead.

Northumberland proposed that he hold the position on the ridge near Sutton Cheney, and Richard agreed to his suggestion. Norfolk moved out along the top of the ridge toward Ambien Hill, Richard and his men followed; they could see along the western extremity of Ambien Hill the three camps of the enemy. Lord Stanley's men were on foot, Sir William's were mounted: Henry Tudor's army had been taken by surprise and were hastily moving east from their camp to interpose the swamp on the south side of Ambien Hill between it and Richard's army occupying the summit.

Norfolk arranged his troops in the shape of a bow facing south-west toward the rebel camp, with the archers on the left facing south toward the swamp. Men-at-arms were placed at the centre, and archers on the right, facing west toward Shenton.

The enemy trumpets sounded. The west wing of the swamp was under the command of the Earl of Oxford. Norfolk's archers let off a volley of arrows and were met with a similar response. Stone cannonballs bombarded the upper slopes. These came from artillery that the rebels had been supplied with by Charles VIII of France, as well as the artillery captured at Shrewsbury. The fact that Sir Richard Guilford had been made Henry's Master of the Ordnance on 8 August indicates that they already had guns when they landed at Milford Haven. Richard, however, had not brought any cannon from the arsenal that he had gathered in the Tower. Richard's men replied to Henry's with guns and serpentines, but they were few in number. The foot soldiers panned round the swamp until they reached a part almost halfway across the base of the hill. Their right flank rested on the swamp, the left was stranded unless it was supported by Sir William's cavalry. Now the rebels shifted position to face Norfolk.

Henry Tudor had about 5,000 men – William Stanley commanded 2,500 and Lord Stanley between 3,000 and 4,000 of these – but still Richard outnumbered him two to one, commanding roughly 9,000 men, of which 3,000 were under Norfolk's command. Richard despatched scouts to ascertain where Henry Tudor was positioned.

The rebel troops began to climb the hill, the royal army plunged down and they collided halfway. Norfolk's ranks were the thinner and there was pressure on the centre where Oxford headed a massive phalanx, so Richard sent reinforcements. Norfolk's tactics now bore fruit and Oxford pulled his men back; a lull fell upon the field. Oxford then gave an order for his men to come in to close formation. He resumed his attack upon Norfolk. Vergil says, '[The Earl] collected his squadrons together and attacked the enemy on one side.'[9]

In effect Oxford was placing all his strength on Henry's left wing; the sources imply that this was when the battle swung around and Richard's men were fighting with the sun in their eyes. Norfolk's earlier advantage was soon lost.

A messenger rode up and told Richard that Henry Tudor's position had been located, however the messenger also bore less pleasant news; John Howard and the Duke of Norfolk had both been slain. Immediately Richard sent for Northumberland, but the traitor now showed his true colours, saying that he thought it best to remain in the rear to guard against a sudden attack from Lord Stanley, and he urged Richard to flee the battle. The battle was less than half an hour old, many of Richard's reserve had not yet been committed and the Stanleys still remained impassive when Richard made the extraordinary decision to seek out Henry Tudor. Maybe his intention was to cut off the head of the rebellion, for once Tudor was dead there would be nothing left to fight for, but whatever his reason, this was a fateful decision. He mounted his horse and cried, 'We go to seek Henry Tudor.' Armed with a battleaxe he moved forward at a walk, the 200 men of the household pacing behind. He rode north-west down the slope to swing clear of the northern battle line, and with less than 100 men Richard charged.

Richard rode straight past Stanley's front and up a slight slope, heading straight toward a milling mass of horsemen. The ranks of Henry's guard surged forward. Sir John Cheney blocked Richard's path, they clashed and Richard despatched him with his battleaxe. Lovell and Robert Percy managed to draw close to Richard's side. Richard was hacking his way toward the standard of the red dragon borne by William Brandon. Richard caught a glimpse of Henry, but he had already reached Brandon, and both the standard bearer and the standard yielded under Richard's axe. His men made a tight arc about their king as they hacked their way closer and closer to Henry. A squire seized Richard's bridle and pointed. Richard turned and saw the red jackets of Sir William Stanley's cavalry hurtling toward them. The *Life* says,

Rhys ap Thomas who from the beginning closely followed the Earl [Henry] seeing his party began to quail, and the

King's gain ground, took this occasion to send to Sir William Stanley, giving him to understand the danger they were in, and entreating him to join their forces for the disengaging of the Earl, who was not only in despair of victory, but almost of his life. Whereon (for it did not seem he understood the danger before) Sir William Stanley made up to Rhys ap Thomas, and joining both together rushed in upon their adversaries.

Another squire brought Richard a fresh horse and Richard spurred it forward with only a few men accompanying him. Richard was getting closer to Henry but his men were falling fast. He cried, 'Treason, treason' as he swung his battleaxe, moving ever forward. None of his household remained at his side; he was beating about him against spears and swords. Finally the blows rained down on him. It seems that Richard had lost his helmet, as well as his horse, at this moment, for recent forensic evidence on his skull implies the blows came from above (i.e. from men on horseback). Although he had received many head injuries, the final fatal blow was yet to come: 'Rhys ap Thomas slew Richard manfully fighting with him hand to hand.' (*Life*)

On 22 August at Bosworth the last Plantagenet king of England was slain. The supreme accolade of being the man who struck the killing blow to Richard was given to Rhys by the poet Guto'r Glyn in his praise poem, which says that 'Rhys killed the boar, destroyed his head'.[10] This is confirmed by the Burgundian writer Jean Molinet, who noted that a Welshman delivered the killing stroke with a halberd while Richard's horse was stuck in the marsh of the battlefield.[11]

Some of Richard's followers managed to escape, including Viscount Lovell and Humphrey Stafford. On the news of the death of the king his army quickly disbanded. Some headed north-east toward Cadeby, some south through the swamp to Redmore Plain, where the victors had gathered. Northumberland remained where he was until he was summoned to Henry, to whom he paid homage, but he was taken into custody. Sir William Stanley retrieved the crown from Richard's battered helmet and placed it upon Henry's head; all knelt and did homage to the new king.

The battle had lasted a mere two hours, with only one hour spent in actual combat. In the afternoon Henry entered Leicester in triumph, followed later by the body of Richard, 'stark naked, despoiled and derided, with a felon's halter about the neck'.[12] The bloody body was slung contemptuously across a horse, which one of the dead king's heralds was forced to ride. As it made its way across the west bridge of the Soar, his head was carelessly battered against the stone parapet. For two days the body was kept on display in the house of the Grey Friars, then he was given a quick burial.

The day after the battle John Sponer rode into York bringing news of Richard's death to the mayor and aldermen: 'It was showed ... by John Sponer ... that King Richard late mercifully reigning upon us was ... piteously slain and murdered, to the great heaviness of this city.[13] The final tribute to the last Plantagenet king came from the men who knew him best.

As a postscript, in 2013, the dramatic discovery of Richard's remains in a car park in Leicester (of which more will be said in a later chapter) shed light on the death of the king. Of the many battle wounds that he had received, the killing blow was dealt to the back of the skull by a 'medieval pole weapon' (halberd). Such a weapon Rhys ap Thomas employed, so there can be little doubt that it was Rhys who dealt the death blow. The man who killed Richard III was now about to achieve greater prominence and favour than he could ever have imagined from his grateful new liege, Henry Tudor, as a new era in British history was about to begin.

4

The Red Rose Restored
(1485–1499)

Within the space of two hours the fortunes of both Henry Tudor and Rhys ap Thomas had changed dramatically. At the Battle of Bosworth, Rhys's aid had played a significant role in gaining Henry what he most desired – the crown of England. Rhys's forces had numbered around 1,000 to 2,000 men and had included a number of landowners and officials from Carmarthenshire and Cardiganshire. A good number of these Welshmen were now rewarded by the new king with offices in the principality or lordship of Kidwelly. Henry also honoured his promise to Rhys that he would make him Chief Governor of South Wales. With the exception of Henry's uncle Jasper, no one else received such commanding authority in South Wales; 'afterward when he had obtained the kingdom he [Henry] gave liberally to Rhys'.[1]

Henry was quick to recognise Rhys's military prowess, but especially the influence that he held in South and West Wales, along with an unswerving loyalty that had been a crucial factor in determining the outcome of Bosworth. Rhys was a man 'noted for strength of will and military expertise … an excellent leader in war'.[2] His motto, '*Secret et Hardi*', can be seen today on the garter plate in St George's Chapel in Windsor.

Tradition says that Henry looked on him as a father figure, affectionately calling him 'Father Rice' despite Rhys being only seven or eight years older, and Henry greatly valued his counsel. Three days after the Battle of Bosworth Henry dubbed Rhys a knight:

> And today is declared a Knight
> And his raven and his shield – line by line –
> To Harry the King power is long given.[3]

Henry's most immediate action after the victory was naturally to secure his throne. He declared himself king retroactively, dating the first day of his reign from 21 August (the day before Bosworth), which thereby rendered all those who had fought for Richard, traitors. This meant that Henry could legally confiscate the lands and property of Richard III. The bill was very unpopular and many spoke against it. The *Croyland Chronicle*, the most comprehensive, if sometimes unreliable, source for the medieval period said, 'O God! What security shall our Kings have henceforth that in the day of battle they may not be deserted by their subjects.' However, Henry also offered a general pardon to those who had fought on the opposing side and in particular he spared Richard's heir, the Earl of Lincoln (John de la Pole).[4]

Henry was crowned on 30 October with much pomp, but there was a scarcity of nobility in attendance. By dividing the power of the nobility through use of bonds and recognisances he had hoped to secure some form of loyalty. He enacted laws against livery and maintenance, which was a lord's practice of having large numbers of retainers who wore the lord's badge or uniform and who could potentially form a private army. By these means he sought to secure his position as monarch. Henry also appointed his counsellors at this time. They comprised his uncle Jasper Tudor; the Duke of Bedford; the earls of Oxford, Shrewsbury and Derby; Richard, Bishop of London; Richard, Bishop of Norwich; Sir Rhys ap Thomas and Morgan of Kidwelly.

That autumn Henry also enhanced Rhys's public authority in the region. The Marcher lordship of Edward Stafford, Duke of Buckingham, was at his disposal during the young Duke's minority. On 3 November Rhys was given supreme authority in Brecon as the king's lieutenant and steward of the lordship, and constable of Brecon Castle – for life. Three days later one of the two most senior offices in the royal shires of Carmarthenshire and Cardiganshire also came his way. On 6 November he was appointed Chamberlain of South Wales for life; this gave him complete control of all the wealth and resources of the two shires, and even though Jasper Tudor was appointed Justiciar of South Wales a month later, it was Rhys who had effective charge of the southern part of the principality.

The poet Lewis Glyn Cothi wrote to Jasper Tudor and offered the following advice:

Take, Wales knows well your lineage,
The raven into your secrets
The fitting swallow [Henry VII] and ravens
Will bring splendour to London.[5]

Rhys governed well, the *Life* tells us,

whenever delinquents were brought before him, his fashion was to begin with gentle words and persuasions seasoning them ever and anon with comfortable admonitions out of the scriptures, so to imprint in the hearts of the offenders the love of justice and honesty, when this was done the party was dismissed. Again if that brought nothing, he would grow more rough, taking to menaces; lastly if all failed and they persevered in ill doing remaining stiff and incorrigible, he either cut them off with the sword of justice, or carried them to the wars there to end them, or amend them.

Life

At Easter, just eight months after Bosworth, insurrection reared its ugly head. It broke out in two areas, first around Worcester, led by Humphrey and Thomas Stafford, and second in the North under Viscount Lovell and other friends of Richard III. It appears that the North would have risen up against Henry on the death of Richard and proclaimed Lincoln as Richard's heir, but Henry put out a false report of Lincoln's death, so without a focus for their rebellion they desisted.

A small force under Jasper Tudor (and possibly Rhys ap Thomas) headed north, offering pardons for those who would take them. By the time they entered York the rebellion had fizzled out, simply because the rebels lacked a leader to challenge Henry's crown. Viscount Lovell made a vain attempt to seize the king, and then went into hiding. The Staffords fared less well; after failing to rally Worcester, they sought sanctuary near Oxford, only to be dragged out by Henry's men. Humphrey was summarily executed while Thomas was pardoned, no doubt because of his connection with Henry's mother.

The first of the rebellions had been quashed relatively easily, and in September that year Henry's wife gave birth to a son in Winchester who was appropriately christened Arthur. The choice of name invoked the mythical king from whom the two warring houses both claimed descent. Merlin the magician had prophesied that the mythical Arthur would be the result of a union between a red king and a white queen, so the young prince's birth seemed auspicious. It was contrived that the birth would take place in Winchester, legendary home of Camelot, and on 20 September 1486 the young Arthur arrived on cue. The bards sang 'Joyous may we be, our prince to see, and roses three.'[6]

However, this did not help alleviate any of the problems that still faced Henry with regard to securing the throne. Richard III had reigned almost eighteen months before he had been subjected to the threat of invasion, and by a strange coincidence Henry had been king almost as long before he too was threatened in the same way. A young man, Lambert Simnel, the ten-year-old son of an Oxford tradesman, had been groomed by Oxford priest Richard Symonds to take on the role of Edward, Earl of Warwick, the son of the Duke of Clarence and Richard's nephew. The real earl, however, was safely locked away in the Tower, but the threat posed to Henry was significant enough, for the man who headed the rebellion was none other than the Earl of Lincoln, Richard's designated heir, and Henry knew that this rebellion was intended to put Lincoln, not Warwick, on the throne.

Symonds took Simnel to Ireland, which was a loyal centre of Yorkist support. The Lord Lieutenant the Earl of Kildare proclaimed Simnel King Edward VI, and he was crowned in

Christ Church Cathedral. They had been joined by the Earl of Lincoln and Viscount Lovell, who had now come out of hiding, and had been seeking support from Richard's sister, Margaret, Dowager Duchess of Burgundy. She provided the means of hiring 2,000 German mercenaries commanded by the reputable soldier Martin Schwartz. On 5 May, Lincoln, Lovell and their troops were triumphantly received in Dublin.

On 4 June Lincoln and his army landed at Furness in Lancashire. They marched across the Pennines, and then they headed south. The people did not rally as he hoped – probably this was because they were suspicious of the Irish soldiers and mercenaries, but also because they may have feared the start of another civil war. On 16 June at East Stoke the two armies met. Lincoln's numbered around 8,000 men while Henry had 12,000. Sir Rhys was with the king, and Lewis Glyn Cothi says that Rhys's bastard brother John, a skilled soldier, was also with him that day.

> When in the battle attacks were made
> On the ravens and them and the King
> John, the steel breasted was not
> Idle there at the fight[7]

The king also had with him the earls of Oxford and Shrewsbury, as well as Lord Strange. The king bestowed a troop of horses on Rhys, no doubt because he had been supressing the rebellion in the North with Jasper Tudor and had not been able to get back to Wales to recruit his own men. 'This favour among the many he received from his gracious master Sir Rhys held or the greatest as being the means whereby the English and the Welsh were forever after tied in an indissoluble kind of true affection.' (*Life*)

The battle lasted three hours and initially Lincoln's forces had the upper hand, as the German soldiers under Schwartz proved effective. Rhys was caught in the thick of the fray, battling almost single-handedly. While he was in hand-to-hand combat with the Earl of Kildare he was hit by an arrow, and 'he would have lost his life had not the Earl of Shrewsbury rescued him out of the hands of the merciless rabble.' (*Life*)

However, Henry's army held firm, and at the end Lincoln, Schwartz, Broughton and the Irish leader Thomas Geraldine were all killed, along with over half of Lincoln's troops. When news reached Henry of Rhys's wounds he sent for him and said, 'How now Father Rice? How like you of the entertainment here? Whether there is better eating leeks in Wales or shamrock among the Irish?' 'Both certainly but coarse fare,' said Rhys, 'yet either would seem a feast with such a companion', pointing at the Earl of Shrewsbury.' (*Life*)

Richard Symonds was arrested and sentenced to life imprisonment in a bishop's prison. On the other hand, Henry was merciful to Lambert Simnel, to whom he gave a position in the king's kitchen, and later the post of king's falconer. Those nobles who had supported Lincoln, twenty-eight of them in total, were all attained and their estates confiscated, adding greatly to Henry's coffers.

The situation in Europe at this time was also changing. Louis XI had extended the frontiers of France by conquering the duchy of Burgundy and had brought all the other independent fiefs under his rule, with the exception of Brittany. When Louis died his daughter, Anne of Beaujeu, and her husband acted as regents to his successor, Charles VIII, until he reached his majority. At roughly the same time the other major European power, the Hapsburg Holy Roman Emperor Fredrick III, withdrew to Linz, leaving his son Maximilian to take over the government.

In the summer of 1488 Henry offered aid to Francis II of Brittany, who was being threatened by France. This was not an altruistic gesture on Henry's part, but was prompted mainly by the fear that France was overreaching herself and that England could well lose command of the Channel if France controlled the Breton coast. Henry sent three vessels and a company of volunteers under Lord Scales to Brittany. However, Duke Francis acceded to terms with the Regent of France, thereby making himself a vassal of Charles VIII, and pledged that his daughter and heiress Anne would not marry without his consent. The following month the duke died and Charles demanded the wardship of Anne. Early in 1491 Maximilian had renewed his suit to marry Anne and with Henry's encouragement they had been married by proxy, but on 6 December she married Charles VIII and he was busy working to make the earlier marriage invalid.

Henry was affronted and immediately cut all diplomatic ties with France, refusing to have any dialogue with the French ambassadors. He summoned Parliament and declared his intention to resurrect the claims of previous English kings to the crown of France. He then began to raise an army of 25,000 foot soldiers and 1,500 cavalry under the command of Jasper, Earl of Bedford; the Earl of Oxford; the Marquis of Dorset; the earls of Derby, Shrewsbury, Suffolk, Devonshire, Kent and Essex and Sir Rhys ap Thomas, the only gentleman to be mentioned among the peers.

Rhys was among the first to assemble at Winchester with a retinue of Welshmen 500 strong ready to cross the Channel and besiege Boulogne. Rhys's contract provided for a force of six men-at-arms with pages, 250 demi-lances and 260 infantry, who were to serve overseas for a year in the first instance, mustering at Winchester on 6 June and receiving expenses from their homes and a month's wages in advance before embarking at Portsmouth. It transpired that the retinue consisted of twelve lances, 286 demi-lances and 292 archers, who were paid for one month from 20 October. However, as soon as the army was ready Henry sailed for Calais, 'rather to show war than to make it'. From here the army marched to Boulogne, where they laid siege to the city for nearly a year.

Henry was, however, hampered in executing his plans for the Breton expedition, because the war taxation had resulted in a rebellion in Yorkshire where a mob had slain the Earl of Northumberland. The English garrison at Calais had done great service to Henry's Burgundian ally in rescuing his troops at Dixude from Flemish rebels, however in an about-face Maximilian signed a separate peace treaty with France, leaving England stranded. Nevertheless, a show of force by Henry had been sufficient and Charles offered him a treaty, which was signed at Etaples on 3 November, allowing the English and Welsh to withdraw on advantageous terms. He was to be handsomely reimbursed for his Breton venture. He received 745,000 ducats and promised a further 25,000 crowns a year for his 'charges sustained in the aid of the Bretons'.[8] Rhys had been one of the captains who had been consulted regarding the terms of the treaty. Nevertheless, it had been a fruitless expedition for the soldiers:

Generally through the whole army they began to speak somewhat broadly of his rapacious disposition, not sticking further to say he cared not whom he polled and pilled to fill his own coffers, with many other reproaches, which the King little heeded, comforting himself with these words; 'The people hiss at me, but I applaud myself at home when I contemplate the amount in the cash box.'[9]

Henry's captains all received lavish presents. Rhys was offered a pension of £700 a year, which he refused, saying that 'if his master intended to relieve his wants then he had sent too little and if to corrupt his mind or stagger his fidelity, his kingdom would not be enough'. It was said that when his men began muttering and mutinying along with all the other soldiers Rhys had done no more than 'hold up his finger and say silent to them and all was hushed such was the reverence they held for him'. (*Life*)

In 1489 Henry approached King Ferdinand and Queen Isabella of Spain regarding a marriage alliance between his son Arthur and the young Catherine, their eldest daughter. In the Treaty of Medina Campo, Henry sought to gain recognition of the establishment of his dynasty, but his troubles were still far from over and his throne still not secure, for in 1491 another pretender to the crown appeared. This time the rebellion would be far more challenging to his long-term security. In early 1490, a young man appeared in Ireland claiming to be the youngest son of Edward IV – Richard, Duke of Gloucester. The young man's name was Perkin Warbeck and he was the son of a poor burgess from Tournai in France. He was employed by a silk merchant and came to Cork with his employer,

1. A portrait of Richard III. An early seventeenth-century copy of an original likeness. (Courtesy of Ripon Cathedral)

2. Henry Tudor, by Holbein. (Courtesy of Elizabeth Norton)

3. Dinefwr Castle. Gruffydd ap Nicholas was deputy constable of this place in 1429. Dinefwr held a special significance for the Gruffydd family.

4. Carmarthen Castle, where Rhys ap Gruffydd was held in 1529 following a disagreement between himself and Lord Ferrers. (Courtesy of Patricia Taylor)

5. Horse harness buckles from Bosworth battlefield. The one on the left bears the arms of Rhys ap Thomas.

6. The site of the Battle of Bosworth Field. (Courtesy of Phil Grain via Amy Licence)

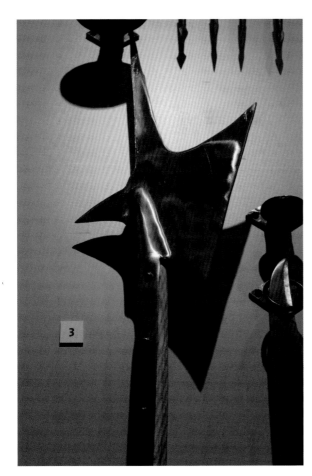

Left: 7. Halberd. (Courtesy of Bosworth Heritage)

Below: 8. Richard's Well, Bosworth Field.

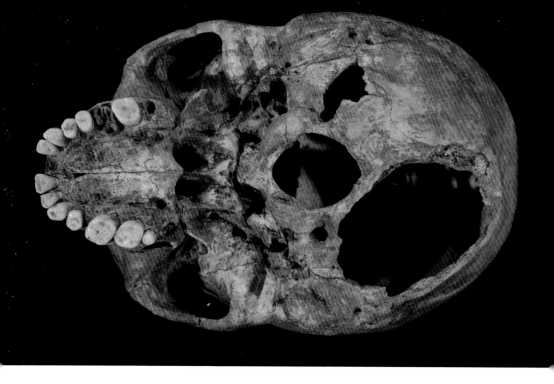

Above: 9. The recently unearthed skull of Richard III, showing several injuries where blows to the head had been made causing his death. The largest of these, on the bottom right, is thought to have been made by a halberd. (Courtesy of the University of Leicester)

Below: 10. A face-on view of the skull of Richard III. (Courtesy of the University of Leicester)

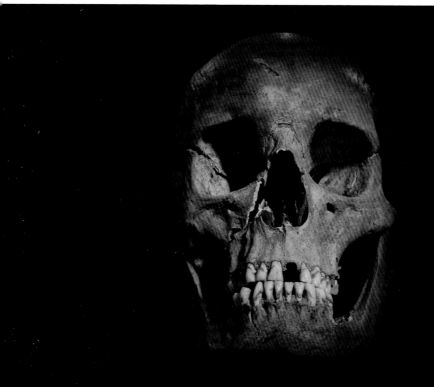

Above: 11. The Great Hall from outside Carew Castle. (Courtesy of Patricia Taylor)

Left: 12. The entrance to the Great Hall, Carew Castle. (Courtesy of Patricia Taylor)

13. Floor tiles showing the arms of Rhys ap Thomas in St Mary's church, Carew. (Courtesy of Patricia Taylor)

14. Inside the Great Hall, Carew Castle. (Courtesy of Patricia Taylor)

Above left: 15. Carew Castle from the mill.

Above right: 16. Entrance to St Peter's church, Carmarthen.

17 & 18. The tomb of Rhys ap Thomas, St Peter's church, Carmarthen. (Courtesy of Patricia Taylor)

where he was mistaken for the Earl of Warwick. Warbeck denied this and instead declared that he was Richard, Duke of York. The story seems highly implausible and clearly this was an elaborate plot engineered by important people with a specific agenda. Warbeck later said 'and so against my will they made me to learn English and taught me what I should do and say'.[10]

It would appear that the Earl of Desmond was chief among the schemers, but soon there was support from France and Scotland, more especially from Margaret, Dowager Duchess of Burgundy, Edward IVs sister. When Warbeck moved on to Flanders he was openly welcomed by Margaret as her nephew, putting Henry in an even more precarious situation. Added to this was the fact that Maximilian promptly recognised Warbeck as the rightful king and this put added pressure on Henry. For if he could not provide any evidence for the death of the young prince then Warbeck's claim, in some eyes, could well be a valid one. If nothing else, it would provide a rallying point for the many disaffected Yorkists in the realm.

When Henry learned of Warbeck's claims and the fact that he intended to sail from Cork to invade the Cornish coast he wrote to the Mayor of Waterford, adding as a postscript in his own hand,

Over this we pray you put you in effectual diligence for the taking of the said Perkin, and him so taken, to send unto us, wherein you shall not only singularly please us, but shall also for the same in money content the sum of 1000 marks sterling for your reward where you may verily trust; for so we assure you by these present letters; and therefore we think it beholding that you set forth ships to the sea for the taking of Perkin aforesaid; for they that take him, and bring him or send him surely unto us, shall have undoubtedly the said reward.[11]

They did not hand Warbeck over, but at least the attempted invasion was halted. In 1492 Warbeck was received by Charles VIII in Paris, where around 100 supporters of the House of York gathered around him; he then moved on to Flanders. Warbeck gained further support from the Emperor Maximilian, who recognised him as Richard IV of England. Henry perceived this as a definite threat to his crown and promptly broke off all trade with Flanders. This was potentially damaging to England, for the cloth trade with Flanders was worth a great deal to the English economy.

Charles, however, soon lost interest in Warbeck, for he had his sights firmly set on the acquisition of northern Italy, which he finally invaded in 1494. Henry had set up an extensive spy network throughout England and Europe, where he discovered that support for Warbeck was not as strong as it had first appeared, but perhaps a more important piece of information gleaned from his informants was the information concerning those who had been supporting Warbeck's cause in England. In 1495, Acts of Attainder were passed by Parliament, including one for Sir William Stanley, who now held the position of chamberlain. He was executed and his estates passed to the king. Lord Fitzwater, Henry's steward, was also executed, but one of those named as plotting against Henry, Sir Robert Clifford, was pardoned and given a reward. It transpired that he had been one of Henry's spies all along.

In June of the same year the planned invasion by Warbeck received the backing of the Emperor Maximilian. Warbeck's fleet appeared off the coast of East Kent at Deal. Henry had prepared for this and his men lay waiting in the sand dunes. When the advance party of Warbeck went ashore they were promptly massacred. Warbeck's ships took flight, vanishing without trace, and no one, not even Henry, could locate his whereabouts. Later that year he suddenly appeared at the court of King James IV of Scotland. It seems that James found a useful purpose for the pretender, for he showered him with gifts, including a pension of £1,200 a year and other favourable attentions. He even married him to Katherine Gordon, a lady of high rank and a coincidently a distant relative of Henry. James set Warbeck up as King of England and in September 1496 headed an army south into English territory. The army encountered strong resistance as they burned, looted and pillaged their way along, but after six days the expedition petered out. It is quite possible that James had no real intention of invading, but was merely using Warbeck as an excuse to flex his muscles against the new Tudor monarch.

Henry was furious; the following month his council began drawing up plans for a military offensive against the Scots. He was given a loan of £120,000 to be repaid by taxation. Martial law was declared, border garrisons were bolstered and Swiss and German mercenaries were recruited in Flanders. By the late spring of 1497 men, horses, carts and ammunition streamed northward toward the Scottish border. Once again, Henry's plans were thwarted, for there was trouble in south-west England. In the face of strong opposition Henry's tax gatherers had been busy filling the coffers, but in the small Cornish parish of St Keverne they met with a disgruntled force. A man named Michael Joseph, who was known by the locals as An Gof the

Blacksmith, accused one of the tax collectors of corruption and refused to pay. This caused a rebellion led by An Gof and a local lawyer Thomas Flamank, which grew and thousands joined their cause as they marched on London. Such was the impact of the threatened invasion that the queen, Henry's mother Margaret Beaufort, and the royal children were moved into the Tower for safety.

The rebels skirted the capital and made camp at Blackheath to make their preparations for a final assault. Henry immediately deployed the army that was en route to Scotland to face the rebels, for as one writer said, 'If the King had lost he would have been finished off and beheaded.'[12] The army was divided into three components; the first was led by the Earl of Oxford, assisted by the earls of Essex and Suffolk, Sir Rhys ap Thomas and Sir Humphrey Stanley. They occupied the hill on the right and left sides to intercept the rebel's passage and take away any chance of flight. The second was under the command of Lord Daubney, who faced the front, and the third remained with the king to provide fresh supplies as and when they may be needed.

Rhys's contribution to the battle cannot be underestimated. He supplied forty-one lances and 696 demi-lances, one tenth of the entire vanguard under the command of Lord Daubney. Rhys's retinue made up the backbone of the king's forces and he received a total payment of £382 16s 0d. On 17 June Rhys deployed his archers and cavalry to outflank the rebels and put them to flight, and for this his retinue was paid £239 8s 4d 'for its trouble'. The Cornish rebels put up a brave fight but Rhys performed the duty of a right noble valiant and redoubted chieftain; for having his horse twice slain under him, and mounted on a third, called Grey Fetter Locks, he made through the thickest of the enemy to Lord Audley, whom after a fierce encounter was his good luck to take, and present to the King as his prisoner, for which brave exploit the King gave him by way of a reward the goods of the said Lord, and withal for his more honour, created him Banneret in the field, having then many wounds about him, scarce bound up bloody from the enemy.[13]

The claim that Rhys personally apprehended James Tuchet, Lord Audley, cannot be substantiated, but instrumental in his capture was a fellow Welsh esquire from Carmarthenshire, William Thomas of Aberglasney, who also seized Audley's brother, so it is highly likely that Rhys was present alongside his own men.

Peace was finally concluded between Scotland and England. Henry offered James his eldest daughter Margaret in marriage, which for James was a much more advantageous prospect than supporting Warbeck, so he threw the pretender out of his country. Warbeck returned to Ireland, where he soon received petitions from the disgruntled people in Cornwall, telling him that they still supported his cause and would be ready to rise up on his behalf. Warbeck hastened with 'six or seven score of his wicked adherents' to England.[14] He landed at Whitsand Bay and from there made his way to Bodmin, where he was welcomed by a throng of 3,000 people. Styling himself Richard IV, he led his people to Exeter, where they laid siege to the city.

Henry immediately sent troops to relieve the town under the command of Lord Brooke, Lord Daubney and Rhys ap Thomas.

When Warbeck received news that Rhys's army was on the way, such was the man's fearsome reputation that Warbeck fled toward Beaulieu in the New Forest, where he went into sanctuary. Henry had commanded Rhys with his troop of 500 cavalry to apprehend him, but he was too late, for Warbeck had already fled, so Rhys staked out the sanctuary until he heard from the king. Henry appeared to be merciful and had Warbeck removed under armed guard and taken to London, where he was paraded in the court as a curiosity. However in June 1498 Warbeck escaped to the Charterhouse at Sheen, where once again he claimed sanctuary; the following day he was handed over to the royal guards. He was publically pilloried in London and then moved to the Tower, where the other threat to Henry's throne, the Earl of Warwick, a young man now in his twenties, was also ensconced.

The danger to the crown was still not over, for in 1499 yet another plot was uncovered when a young student from Cambridge, Ralph Wilford, was groomed by a priest to pose as the Earl of Warwick. The plot was swiftly dealt with, and Wilford was brought to London and hanged. The whole episode was highly traumatic for Henry, and it started to take a heavy toll on his health. In the months that followed Wilford's execution Henry summoned a Welsh priest who had foretold the deaths of Edward IV and Richard III. The priest advised him that his life was in danger and that there were 'two parties of very different political creeds' in the kingdom, indicating that Yorkist conspiracies were still rife.[15]

By the middle of the year royal agents had picked up rumours of plots incriminating four of Warbeck and Warwick's warders, whom, it appears, were acting as go-betweens. The plot was due to be hatched in the summer while London was quiet and the king was on progress. Warbeck and Warwick were encouraged to participate and of the two, Warwick seemed the most enthusiastic. By the end of August, when the conspirators met for the final time, the net closed in. The sentence was death, and on 23 November 1499 Warbeck was taken for execution. He was lashed to a wooden hurdle and hanged on the scaffold at Tyburn. He confessed to being a foreigner from Tournai, not the Duke of York, and begged the king's pardon.

By comparison, the trial of the Earl of Warwick was a farce. He gave his accusers every assistance at his court appearance, and the mere fact that he was backward and had been imprisoned with little or no company for fourteen years should have suggested that he had merely been flattered by the conspirators rather than being an active supporter, but this did nothing to mitigate his sentence. Five days after Warbeck's execution, Warwick was beheaded on Tower Green. Henry had finally removed all possible Plantagenet contenders to the throne. After ruling for fifteen years, only now could Henry start to feel secure.

5
Festivals and Farewells
(1500–1509)

Throughout the tumultuous period of the 1490s Henry did not forget those who had served him well during this time, and none had benefited more than Rhys ap Thomas. When Jasper Tudor died on 21 December 1495 Rhys was appointed Chief Justiciar of South Wales, an appointment that was made by the young Prince Arthur. Later in 1502, on the death of William Devereux, he obtained the constableship of Aberystwyth Castle for life, whose garrison numbered twelve archers. Henry's trust and affection for Rhys cannot be underestimated, and is reflected on a private level as well as from the public honours he received. Rhys was asked to oversee the building of a new tomb for the body of Henry's father, Edmund Tudor, Earl of Richmond. Around 1496 Henry assigned £43 10s from the clerical subsidy collected in the archdeacons of St David's and Cardigan for the 'making of a new tomb for our most dear father' and part of an annual gift of alms to the Grey Friars church in Carmarthen where Edmund Tudor had been buried.

Rhys was handed the money and was responsible for commissioning the tomb chest in Purbeck marble. It survived the Dissolution of the Monasteries and was later transferred to St David's Cathedral in Pembrokeshire.[1] On an even more personal level was the despatch from Rhys to the king of quantities of metheglin, the spiced mead that was a speciality of Wales and for which Henry had acquired a fondness, as well as for hawks and falcons.

The early part of the new century was a time of peace, the country was free from internal strife and celebrations were the order of the day. The marriage between Prince Arthur and Catherine of Aragon, which had been brokered by Henry two years earlier, finally took place on 14 November 1501, the ceremony being held at St Paul's Cathedral. Princess Catherine was accompanied by the ten-year-old Prince Henry, Arthur's younger brother. The walls of the cathedral were hung with fine tapestries and the high altar bedecked with gold plate, ornaments, and relics encrusted with precious stones. An elevated walkway from the west door was covered in red cloth and stretched the entire length of the cathedral – sixty feet long. The king, queen, and the king's mother Margaret Beaufort concealed themselves in a closet adjoining the stage where the ceremony would take place, so they could 'apperceive the form and manner of the ministration'.[2]

Prince Arthur approached the stage by a side door, then Prince Henry handed the bride to his brother. So began the three-hour-long ceremony. When it was over Arthur left by the same side door by which he had entered, to meet Catherine at the Bishop of London's palace, and Catherine and Prince Henry went back the way they had arrived. The wedding feast continued until five in the evening, and was followed by drinking and entertainments. The next day, forty barges conveyed the royal party and some dignitaries 2 miles downstream to Westminster, where spectacular jousts had been arranged, much to the delight of the onlookers. In the evening the entertainments continued in Westminster Hall, with the young Prince Henry stealing the show by discarding his robes to dance with his sister in his jacket, much to the amusement of his parents.

After a week of festivities, the party moved to Richmond, 8 miles upriver. Richmond was a red-brick palace that Henry had designed as a testament to his new dynasty. It boasted onion-shaped domes and glass-filled bay windows, pleasure gardens and most surprisingly of all, plumbing. The festivities continued until the 29 November, culminating with a flock of white doves being released in the great hall the night before. A few days later the young couple left for Ludlow in the Welsh Marches, Prince Arthur's seat.

Meanwhile, back in Wales, Rhys had also been busy making marriage alliances for his children, the majority of which were illegitimate. Nonetheless, Rhys sought the best possible matches he could find and many were willing to forego that slight impediment in order to marry into the illustrious family of Rhys ap Thomas. He made the best match for his legitimate son and heir Gruffydd, to Catherine St John, daughter of John St John of Bletsoe in Bedfordshire and of Fynnon and Pen-marc in Glamorgan. The marriage would most likely have had the personal approval of Henry, for Catherine was his kinswoman. She was the great-granddaughter of Margaret Beauchamp, whose second husband was John Beaufort, Duke of Somerset, who was the father of Margaret Beaufort, Henry's mother. Rhys had won the king's trust and regard to a high degree, and consequently now saw his son given a position in the prince's household, as well as a bride with royal lineage. It is also possible that Margaret Beaufort may have played a significant role in promoting this union, for Catherine's brother John grew up in her household and it is highly likely that Catherine had also grown up under her watchful eye.

However, this was not the only royal connection in the family, for Rhys's second wife, Dame Jenet Matthew, was the first cousin of Catherine's grandmother, Elizabeth Matthew, whose grandmother was the daughter, strangely enough, of Gruffydd ap Nicholas, which also made Rhys a distant cousin of Elizabeth Matthew. The marriage of his son took place sometime during Gruffydd's service with Prince Arthur, for by 1508 they had produced a second child, a son and heir, Rhys ap Gruffydd.

On 5 April 1502, just five months after the wedding of Arthur and Catherine, a messenger arrived at the palace bearing bad news for Henry. His son had died, presumably of the sweating sickness that had been rife that year. Henry and Elizabeth were distraught, not only through natural grief at the loss of a child, but also because it raised questions about the security of the succession. They had one heir left, Prince Henry, but he was only ten years old, and this recalled the ugly spectre of yet another young prince who had been the sole heir to the Yorkist dynasty. Should anything happen to Henry then the political implications could indeed be disastrous.

Rhys's eldest and only legitimate son, Gruffydd, was a member of Arthur's household by the time the prince married Catherine of Aragon of Spain in November 1501. When Arthur died, it appears that Gruffydd was with him at Ludlow. He played a prominent part in the funeral procession, which made its way to the prince's final resting place before the high altar at

Worcester Cathedral on 23 April. Catherine did not accompany her husband's funeral cortege because she was also ill, so she was taken directly to London. According to the account of one of the heralds concerning the funeral procession, Sir Gruffydd, with an officer at arms on either side, 'in mourning rode on a courser trapped with black'.³ His master's death greatly affected Gruffydd, for when Gruffydd died in 1521 he was also buried in Worcester Cathedral, presumably at his own request. His tomb chest, which his father probably commissioned, stands in the eastern transept, close to the chantry chapel that Henry VII erected to his son. The tomb chest has affinities with that of Edmund Tudor in St David's, and is likewise made from Purbeck marble.

Throughout the wedding festivities Henry had been plagued by yet another pretender to the throne, Edmund de la Pole, the Duke of Suffolk. He was the younger brother of John de la Pole, the Earl of Lincoln, and both were nephews of Richard III, thereby giving them a strong claim to the throne. The recent execution of the Earl of Warwick, Suffolk's cousin, brought home to him the realisation of his own family's entitlements. Henry had already been warned by his counsellors that Suffolk would cause him much distress and that he would 'engineer some dangerous assault against the state'.⁴ Just before the wedding festivities, Suffolk had fled the country, heading toward Austria at the invitation of the Holy Roman Emperor, Maximilian. Although sympathetic to Suffolk's cause, Maximilian could not offer open assistance because of the treaty between his son, Philip of Burgundy, and Henry, nevertheless he told Suffolk that he was welcome to stay, have safe passage throughout the Imperial territories and guaranteed military backing.

Suffolk had a small group of supporters, including Sir George Neville, Sir Thomas Wyndham and the Tyrell family, who provided the link in the chain of conspiracy to Calais. Henry opened negotiations with Maximilian, sending Sir Charles Somerset and William Warham to the emperor, but he gave little response to their requests. News reached Henry that just before Suffolk had fled, he had hosted a private dinner, and the guests had included Thomas Grey, the young Marquis of Dorset; the Earl of Essex and Lord William Courtney, heir to the Earl of Devon. It appeared that a conspiracy was afoot, but the stories were so convoluted that it was difficult to unravel the truth.

In Calais Henry ordered Sir Sampson Norton to occupy Tyrell's stronghold of Guisnes, but he failed to do so. In 1502 Sir Thomas Lovell arrived in Calais and managed to persuade Tyrell to accompany him back to England, no doubt offering him an amnesty, but once he had him aboard ship then it became all too clear that this was not going to be the case. Tyrell was imprisoned in the Tower amid rumours that an Imperially backed invasion was imminent, led by Suffolk – the capital was on the alert. In March Sir Reynold Bray swooped on Porchester Castle, where it was believed the garrison had been infiltrated by Suffolk's sympathisers. Various suspects were rounded up and taken to Winchester, where they were beheaded. These were worrying times for Henry, and the death of Arthur only added to the tension, for this was Suffolk's chance to make a move. Suffolk had waited anxiously in Aachen for men and money from Maximilian to finance his invasion, none of which had been forthcoming. He despatched a letter to Maximilian saying,

I have been warned in no uncertain terms, that King Henry is seeking in all places, and through all kinds of people that he can buy off with gold or silver, to destroy me; and moreover that longer I stay out of England, the stronger King Henry will become, and the worse it will be for me.[5]

It finally occurred to Suffolk that Maximilian was probably one of the 'people' taking money off Henry; he could do nothing without men and money. Finally he escaped to Guelders in Flanders to wait for another opportunity.

Following Arthur's death, more arrests were made, including Lord William Courtney and William de la Pole (Edmund's younger brother). In May there was a show trial of James Tyrell, his servant Robert Wellesbourne, Sir John Wyndham and a shipman; they were all hauled before a judicial commission and sentenced to death. Tyrell and Wyndham were beheaded on Tower Green and shortly afterward rumours were spread abroad that Tyrell had confessed to being responsible for the deaths of the Princes in the Tower. Wellesbourne remained imprisoned; he implicated Tyrell's son Thomas, Matthew Jones and Sir Robert Curzon's courier. Jones and the courier were executed. Wellesbourne's testimony had been crucial, and it is possible that he was one of Henry's double agents, for by the end of May he had received a royal pardon and was retained by the king on half a year's salary of 6os 1od. He was definitely in Henry's employ later when he obtained access to Suffolk's confidential correspondence, copying letters and sending them back to Henry.

Another, more personal, blow for Henry was now waiting in the wings. Late in January 1503 Henry and the royal household moved to the Tower, where Queen Elizabeth was about to go into confinement to await the birth of her latest child. On 2 February, only a fortnight into her confinement, Elizabeth went into labour. The whole business was handled badly and Elizabeth had a raging fever. Henry sent messengers throughout the night to get specialists, but it was all to little avail. On 11 February, on her thirty-seventh birthday, Elizabeth died, and her frail daughter who was hastily christened Catherine soon followed. The funeral arrangements were left to Margaret Beaufort, Thomas Howard and Sir Richard Guilford. Henry ordered masses to be said and then 'privily departed to a solitary place to pass his sorrows and would no man should resort to him'.[6] On 22 February Elizabeth's funeral cortege made its way through the silent streets of London toward Westminster Abbey.

Over 4,000 flaming torches lit the processional way; the main streets of Cornhill and Cheapside were lined with white-clad men holding burning brands. Thirty-seven virgins stood at Fenchurch Street all holding lighted tapers. Among the many epitaphs that were hung around Elizabeth's tomb was a poem by Thomas More, spoken as if by the queen herself. The poignant lines 'The year yet launcheth, and lo now here I lie' were indeed an ominous prediction, for Henry was a shattered man and this was a blow from which he never really recovered.

In the summer of the following year, 1503, Henry finally received dispensation from the Pope for the marriage of Catherine, Arthur's widow to the young Prince Henry, and their betrothal took place on the 3 July, closely followed by more executions of conspirators. Yet more matches were made that summer when Henry's eldest daughter Margaret was married to James IV of Scotland. There had been a proxy wedding at Richmond on 25 January, with the Earl of Bothwell standing as proxy for the Scottish king. In August, Henry, his daughter and his retinue set out for Edinburgh, despite Henry being slightly reluctant to let her go, for she was now the heir apparent should anything happen to the young prince.

Polydore Vergil says that many of the English nobility were against the match as it would give the Scots an advantage should anything happen to Prince Henry, and they feared coming under Scottish rule. He said,

> What then? Should anything of the kind happen (and God avert the omen) I foresee that our realm would suffer no harm since England would not be absorbed by Scotland, but Scotland by England, being the noblest head of the entire island, since there is always less glory and honour being joined to that which is for the greater, just as Normandy came under the rule and power of our ancestors to England.[7]

It was a fear that would later be realised after the death of Henry's granddaughter Elizabeth I.

By the time the party had reached Nottingham Henry had received news of the death of Reginald Bray, his chief advisor, so the royal party turned back, reaching the duchy of Lancaster estates on 31 August. Margaret continued the journey, and on 8 August she was married at Holyrood Abbey.

In 1505, news reached England that Suffolk was planning an invasion from Guelders and had amassed 6,000 men. However, the fighting that had commenced in 1502 between the Duke of Burgundy and the Duke of Guelders resumed, and Guelders was captured by Burgundy. Suffolk was now prisoner of the duke in his fortress of Namur in Flanders, and although he was honour bound by his treaty with Henry to hand him over, Burgundy saw that he had a good bargaining ploy. Suffolk was kept on meagre rations with six men guarding him. There was little Henry could do, but in January 1506 a stroke of luck brought Philip of Burgundy to the English court. Philip was on his way to Spain when his ship was wrecked off the Dorset coast. Philip was now the 'guest' of the English king, and Henry would not let him go until he had extracted his promise that Suffolk would be extradited. On 16 March Suffolk was taken to Calais, and from there to London, where he was imprisoned in the Tower. He was interrogated and stripped of his hereditary titles. His brother Richard still remained at large in Europe, but Suffolk was never to leave his confinement; finally, eight years later, he was beheaded by Henry's son, Henry VIII.

In Wales, the peace that now followed the tumultuous years of the later 1490s meant that Rhys ap Thomas could concentrate on governing his territories, but most importantly, the first of his tasks in 1506 was the staging of one of the most splendid tournaments ever seen in the principality, to commemorate his elevation to the Order of the Garter.

The most important honour that Henry bestowed on Rhys was to make him a Knight of the Order of the Garter in 1505. He filled the vacancy left by the death of the king's uncle Viscount Welles. His sponsors were Prince Arthur and some of the king's close advisors who had also fought against the rebels. Rhys was also given the lordship of Narberth:

Now the report goes that when he was accepted of the honour, the Earldom of Pembroke or of Essex was offered him. Notwithstanding he made rather choice to confrere of the order; and being asked whether he preferred a temporary title before what by continuance would enoble his posterity; he made answer that his profession was arms, and the greatest honour that could be conferred upon a soldier, was knighthood. As for his son and his son's son, and for the rest of his posterity, if they were ambitious of further advancement, his desire was for their more glory, they should sweat for the same as he had done.[8]

The festivities were held in his recently acquired castle at Carew, of which the eighteenth-century traveller and writer John Leland says was 'repaired and magnificently built by Sir Rhys ap Thomas'.[9] Sir Rhys reconstructed the medieval hall, which was 81 feet long, on the western side of a long court, as well as an eastern range, with its grand stairway leading to a lesser hall, and probably the entrance and outer gatehouse. Many of the ornamental features still survive, including the great oriel window of the main hall, and the porch, which bear the shields of the royal arms of England, Prince Arthur and Catherine of Aragon. The battlements and turrets were altered for visual effect rather than any military purposes. There were two stable blocks – the one near the river was 128 feet long – and two smithies' forges for shoeing the horses. Rhys lived here in the opulent splendour befitting one of his standing at court. In the vicinity of the castle were extensive parks, which Leland also visited: 'Coming from Lamphey toward Tenby I rode by a ruinous wall of a park sometime [be]longing to Sir Rhys now void of deer. In the park is very little or no high wood, but shrubs and firs, like as in all parks about Carew walled in stones.'[10]

The year following at his investiture Rhys held his 'solemn jousts and festivities' and the guests came from all over Wales to take part, including Rhys's son, Gruffydd ap Rhys. Other notable guests were Sir Thomas Perrot and Sir William Wogan, men of some note and also neighbours. Arnold Butler, Richard Griffith and John Morgan were also in attendance; these men, hardened soldiers, had served Rhys well over the past two decades. In total there were approximately 500 to 600 men attending the tournament; men of distinction were lodged at the castle while tents and pavilions were erected in the parks for those of lesser status:

> For them [the men of lesser status] tents and pavilions were pitched in the park, near to the castle, where they quartered all the time, every man according to his qualities, the place being furnished beforehand, with all sorts of provisions for that purpose.[11]

The festival lasted for five days:

> On St George's eve [21 April] which was the first day of their meeting, Sir Rhys took a view of all the company, choosing out 500 of the tallest and ablest among them; those he divided into five troops a hundred to each troop, over whom he appointed captains, David the younger and John two of his brothers, Arnold Butler, Richard Griffith and John Morgan.

The men were exercised the following day as though they were being prepared to go into battle; the exercises lasted all day. Early on the morning of St George's day the drums beat and the trumpets sounded, and the captains led their men forward in military array. They were followed by Sir Rhys on horseback, with two pages and a herald also on horseback; they in turn were followed by the rest of the company, and they solemnly marched to the Bishop's Palace at Lamphey. When they reached the gates, Sir Rhys 'willed the messenger to assure the Bishop that he was a man of peace, for he came there to pray for St George's soul and for the welfare and safety of his master, sole sovereign of that honourable order, where he was an unworthy companion; in which heart and devoted exercise he earnestly desired the bishop would be pleased to come with him'.[12]

Rhys then went with a company of men to Bishops Park, where he had a tent erected; here, he put on the livery of a knight of St George, then walked, accompanied by a herald and two pages carrying his train, to Bishop's Palace. He was welcomed by the bishop, the Abbot of Talley and the Prior of Carmarthen, and they processed round the court toward the chapel for a service. Following this they returned to Carew for dinner; as they approached the castle a volley was fired by the captains and this salutation was returned from the walls of the castle. Once all the formalities were dispensed with, the troops made their way to the park, where they entertained their soldiers and friends. The more notable men processed with a fanfare of drums and trumpets toward the castle.

In the great hall two large tables were erected. Rhys's son Gruffydd was the server, William Herbert the carver and Griffith of Penryn the cup bearer.

When the meat was brought to the table the bishop stood on the right side of the chair, Rhys on the left, and all the while the meat was laying down, the cornets, hautbois, and other wind instruments were not silent. After the table was served and all set, the bishop made his humble obeisance to the King's chair, and then descended to say grace.

The evening was filled with entertainment and feasting, and later William Herbert stepped forward and challenged all comers to jousts and tournaments the next day 'in honour of the ladies'. Gruffydd immediately took up the challenge, followed by most of the other assembled gentry – Robert Salisbury, Jenkin Mansell, Vaughan of Tretower, Sir Thomas Perrot, Sir William Wogan, and Griffith Dwnn; they decided that Rhys should have the honour of being the judge. The following morning, Rhys 'had on him fair gilt armour; two pages well provided on horseback before him, with a herald and two trumpeters; himself mounted on a goodly steed, richly barbed and trapped, with four footmen, two on each side attending him, two hundred tall men in blue coats, some before and some behind him'. At one end of the tilt was a tent for the challengers and a similar one was placed at the other end for the defendants. Once Rhys had ascertained that all was in order he took his judgement seat, which was positioned somewhere in the middle of the tilt.

The trumpets sounded and the contestants circuited the tilt two or three times, showing their shields to the judge. Then they began the jousts, each pair of combatants running six courses before dismounting and beginning the 'Turney', the combat with swords. Rhys had taken all precautions to ensure that the contestants did not come to any harm by ordering them to be parted by the 'stickes'[13] to make sure that there were no serious injuries.

After all the contestants had taken part and performed with both lances and swords, it then fell to Rhys to make a decision.

[Rhys] after a long arbitration with himself grew doubtful in opinion; for some of them were excellent at the spear, and some at the sword; some who were well with the sword failed with the spear and they that surmounted with the spear fell short with the sword. This bred much difficulty in judgement, so that Sir Rhys to draw the thread even, when first he had commended them for their heroic deeds, and given a large testimony of their skill and valour in the performance of them, concluded in the language of Virgil's Shepherd:

It is not for me to settle so a high a contest between you.
You deserve the heifer, and he also, and whoever shall
Feel the sweetness or taste the bitterness of love.[14]

Willingly them merrily, as you see by way of caution to take heed of those dames, whose honours that day they had so faithfully maintained.'[15]

That evening at supper, Gruffydd, in the presence of his father Rhys, challenged Sir William Herbert, four to four, at the ring the following morning. The forfeit was that the loser would pay for a supper at Carmarthen for a farewell parting. Sir William was happy to join in, but he requested that two young men, the heirs of Penrhyn and Guidir, might be included. The next morning Rhys took his judge's seat and the contest began.

It had been agreed by Rhys and his son that Rhys should award the winning judgement to Sir William's group, so that

Gruffydd could show them the delights of Carmarthen town. After dinner they all went hunting and killed many deer, which would be taken to Carmarthen for the last feast of the festivities. So ended the great festival, which was remembered for a long time by the people of Wales. To mark the occasion two sturdy oak chairs were made, and decorated with his arms enclosed within the garter and its motto. Although the chairs are dated by some experts to around 1520 it is not unreasonable to suggest that they may have been carved locally in South West Wales as part of a set designed for the notable celebrations at Carew in 1506.[16]

Rhys's hospitality to his kinsmen was well remembered, as the *Life* tells us:

Sir Rhys was entertaining a friend to dinner when the brother in law of Sir Rhys came to the house. As the door was not opened to his first knock, he immediately left. The knight, hearing this directed that his brother in law be brought back to the table board saying, 'Bring him back without fail, for he will be deeply offended at having had a locked door at my house.' His servants brought him back and Sir Rhys saw at once that food was placed before him. The knight apologised for the poorness of the fare saying, 'I'm sorry you did not come earlier since there is now very little except bones and sinews. But cheer up we'll make up for it at supper!' The brother in law shrewdly replied, 'What can one expect but bones and sinews where ravens and dogs are found so often!' For Sir Rhys' guest bore dogs and Sir Rhys ravens as arms.[17]

His household was also a magnet for a group of talented poets, who were attracted by his reputation. Most notable among them were the poets Guto'r Glyn, who visited Abermarlais, and Tudur Aled, one of the most esteemed contemporary poets, who visited Rhys in many of his properties in South Wales, ending his days in the Franciscan friary in Carmarthen after having first taken holy orders. There were other poets who did not actually visit Rhys, but who sought to attract his attention and possible patronage with praise poems, no doubt vying with each other to secure his favour. Lewis Glyn Cothi, Siancyn Fynglwyd and Rhys Nanmor all publicised the blood connection between Rhys's family and that of the Tudor line, who both claimed Ednyfed Fychan as an ancestor. More significantly was the stress they laid on Rhys's own accomplishments, from his feats in battle to his election to the Order of the Garter. Dafydd Llwyd was the first to acknowledge his role in the downfall of Richard III.

Iowerth Fyngwld noted the imposing figure he cut among the knights at Sheen, Henry VII's palace in 1497.

> It is unlikely that nine Saxons would give in Sheen
> A challenge to the Raven of Harry the King.[18]

In many of these poems Rhys would be compared to the chivalric knights of legend and it is clear that Rhys certainly saw himself in these terms. The few remaining possessions belonging to the family – the two Garter oak chairs, the oak tester valances from Rhys's bed depicting siege and war against the French, the remnant of an oak cupboard at Cotehele House in Cornwall[19] portraying harpists and the pleasures of the chase – all illustrate the pride, self-confidence and sense of honour that had won him approbation among his contemporaries. No doubt his sense of duty to the chivalric code had been acquired when he was a young man at the court of Burgundy. In fact, so enamoured by knightly deeds was Rhys that he commissioned a copy of the Welsh prose translation of *La Queste del Saint Graal* (the tales of Arthur and the Knights of the Round Table). In fact Rhys's household became one of the most important cultural centres in Wales.

There is no mention in the *Life* of Rhys's activities during the period 1501–9 save that he was busy with his estates, although there is evidence to show that he made several appearances at court and brought Henry gifts. It may have been possible that he was in attendance in December 1508 at the betrothal of Henry's youngest daughter, the fourteen-year-old Mary, to Charles of Castile, through his proxy the Lord of Bergen. This was indeed a coup for Henry, because the Tudor/Hapsburg alliance would mean that Mary would be queen of an empire that spanned Christendom, from the southern tip of Spain to the borders of Poland and Hungary, from Naples to the Netherlands.

Henry's printer, Richard Pynson, who commented upon the wedding festivities, also wrote,

> Thy flourishing red roses be so planted and spread in the highest Imperial gardens and houses of power and honour, that by such buds and branches by God's good grace shall proceed to them, all Christian regions shall hereafter be united and allied unto thee, which honour till now thou could never attain.[20]

There was much rejoicing, and a variety of entertainments lasting two weeks. Meanwhile, Prince Henry's betrothal to his brother's widow Catherine still hung in the balance. This was one marriage that was never to take place during Henry Tudor's lifetime.

In January Henry left for his palace at Hanworth, where once again he fell ill. The symptoms he displayed suggest he was suffering from tuberculosis with the added complication of a bout of quinsy. No doubt fearing that his time was near, in early February he visited the Benedictine abbey at Chertsey, and on his way back stopped at the bishop's palace at Esher, where it is probable that he discussed the possible outcomes of his death, where the dynasty was concerned, with Richard Fox, a man who had been close to him for twenty-five years. There still remained the spectre of a challenge to the throne; although the Earl of Suffolk was firmly incarcerated in the Tower, his brother was still at large in Europe. The Duke of Buckingham also gave the impression that he was ready to make a challenge, or would be ready to offer support to any rival. Perhaps Henry's death would be a signal to make that challenge? This is maybe what Henry feared, more so than his imminent demise. Everyone was now looking to the young Prince Henry to provide reform and to restore the political order. The question for Henry was how to effect a smooth transition for his heir.

By the end of February the royal household moved downriver to Richmond. From that time onwards no one saw the king, and his health remained a closely guarded secret. By the end of March Henry was close to death. He lay amid a mound of pillows, gasping for breath. He mumbled constantly that 'if it pleased God to send him life they should find him a new, changed man'.

The king lasted the month; on 16 April prisoners were released, alms distributed, masses paid for and a general pardon issued – all acts of royal contrition. Henry, it appears, made an exemplary death, his eyes fixed intently on the crucifix. On Saturday 21 April Henry died. On 9 May his funeral cortege wound its way to St

Paul's Cathedral. On top of the coffin, reposing on cloth-of-gold cushions, was a life-size effigy. The following day the coffin was taken to Westminster Abbey, where Henry was buried alongside 'our dearest late wife, the Queen', as he had requested.

The heralds proclaimed for the first time ever in England, 'The King is dead, long live the King', and for the first time the names of the king and his heir were included. The Tudor dynasty had been established and a new Tudor rose was about to come into bloom.

6
King of the Ravens
(1509–1524)

On the death of the king, Rhys had few qualms about what he could expect from the new incumbent. He had served Henry VII faithfully and expected to continue that role under the late king's son, Henry VIII. The new king had acquired a fortune from his miserly father, and for most of the first two years of his reign he spent his time and newly acquired wealth on festivities and revels. In 1509 Henry hurriedly arranged his marriage to Catherine of Aragon, saying that it had been his father's dying wish. Whether this was true or not, it did leave unresolved issues regarding the papal dispensation to marry his dead brother's widow. On the other hand it may just have been a convenient time, because the Holy Roman Emperor Maximilian I had been attempting to marry his granddaughter Eleanor (who was also Catherine's niece), to Henry. The wedding of Henry and Catherine was a low-key affair that took place in the friary church in Greenwich, and on 24 June they held their joint coronation in Westminster Abbey.

Henry was far more lenient than his father had been with regard to some of the Yorkist prisoners who languished in the Tower. Several of them were pardoned, including the Marquis of Dorset. Edmund de la Pole, however, was not among them. Later, in 1513, he was executed because his brother Richard, still at large in Europe, had sided against Henry with the King of France.

Notable among the king's household at this time was Rhys's son Gruffydd, who was now also pursuing a career, entering Lincoln's Inn to learn law on 26 February 1509. On 4 May both Rhys and his son received a general pardon from the king in expectation of future service. There was now no one of the stature of Jasper Tudor that could possibly hinder Rhys's progress in South Wales, and Rhys was soon able to extend his authority southwards from Carmarthenshire and Cardiganshire. His intention was that his son should inherit all these domains after his death, and by doing so he would be able to implement his own dynastic ambitions. On 11 May Rhys was authorised to continue his role as Justiciar of South Wales at the new king's pleasure. By August 1509 Rhys was acting as steward in the lordship of Pembrokeshire; his son became steward of the smaller lordship in south Cardiganshire, which encompassed the eastern half of the commote of Iscoed and the western part of Gwynionydd.

In April 1511 a similar arrangement allowed Rhys's hold on the stewardship of Builth to pass to his son. However, Rhys may have overstepped the mark in his ambitious plans. The one post that had eluded him was the constableship of the royal castle of Carmarthen. During the reign of Henry VII from June 1498, this post had been held by Gruffydd Rede, who came from a prominent local family and who had avidly supported the old king. Henry had rewarded him with the lordship of Kidwelly and later with the stewardship of Pembroke. When in May

1509 Henry VIII made him his steward, receiver, approver and chancellor of the lordships of Pembroke and Haverfordwest, not to mention the barony of Cemais, Rhys may well have felt more than a little aggrieved.

By 9 July, Rede had been murdered. Rhys was not among those named as being present at the deed, but the poet and herald Gruffydd Hireathog recorded that he believed Rhys was actually responsible for the crime. A few months later a rumour spread around London that lent some weight to this accusation. Thomas, Lord Darcy, reported to the Keeper of the Privy Seal, Richard Fox, that 'Sir Rhys had gone to sea, fled the country.' (*Life*)

However, this proved to be a false report and Rhys, undaunted by all the rumours, went on to acquire the stewardship of Pembroke on Rede's death. However, it was another Carmarthen squire, William Thomas, who was preferred over him as constable of Carmarthen Castle. Despite the stain on his otherwise flawless character, Henry needed men such as Rhys. His fighting skills were renowned, despite him now being a man in his sixties. The same could not be said for his son Gruffydd, whose first known exploits in warfare were not auspicious.

At this time, France, in league with the Holy Roman Emperor under a treaty known as the League of Cambrais, was winning a war against Venice. Henry, against some of his council's wishes, renewed his father's friendship with France's king, Louis XII. Shortly afterwards, in an about-face, Henry signed a treaty with Ferdinand of Spain against France. This was helped along in 1511 when the Pope, Julius II, created the anti-French league, known as the Holy League, which brought Louis into conflict with Ferdinand. Henry joined Ferdinand in an initial Anglo-

Spanish attack on Aquitaine. It was planned for the spring and England hoped to recover possession of the duchy.

In 1512 Gruffydd and a retinue of 500 men joined the Marquis of Dorset's army, which was being sent to aid King Ferdinand of Spain in his invasion of Gascony. He received a loan of £333 6s 8d to help finance his retinue and a further £266 13s 4d for his men. Gruffydd was employed as Dorset's councillor, and they set sail from Southampton in early June. Rhys did not take part in this expedition, but he sent some of his men along to swell the ranks. This was probably just as well for Rhys's martial reputation, as the expedition proved to be something of a calamity. The army spent weeks of inactivity in Fuenterrain in northern Spain in deteriorating conditions. Eventually the army abandoned its position and returned home by the end of August. The whole campaign was a failure, for Ferdinand had used this compact merely to further his own ambitions, and this put great strain on the Anglo-Spanish alliance. The French were ejected from Italy shortly afterwards and the alliance managed to survive, both parties wanting victory over the French. Henry finally managed to persuade Maximilian to join the league, and secured from him the promise of the title of 'Most Christian King of France' and possible coronation in Paris by the Pope, if he could defeat Louis. With these prizes dangling tantalisingly before him, Henry invaded France.

This time Gruffydd ap Rhys's role was less prominent, while in 1513 Rhys took pride of place alongside the Earl of Shrewsbury and Sir Charles Somerset in command of the vanguard of the king's army that invaded northern France. On 15 May Rhys raised a large retinue of 3,000 infantry and light cavalry, and in June crossed to Calais. Here, Rhys and his son deposited £3,000 worth of gold, silver and plate with Sir Gilbert Talbot, the Deputy Lieutenant of Calais, for safekeeping. War was an expensive business, for they also had to purchase clothing and war harnesses worth £900 from the king, which they optimistically promised would be repaid by Whitsun 1515.[1]

The chronicler Holinshed says that Shrewsbury, Somerset and Rhys, whom he describes as 'a gentleman of such sport and hardiness that he is named the flower of the Welshmen, as the poet said, *Ricius Thomas flos Cambrabritannum*',[2] marched from Calais for three days, past Sangatte toward Marquise, as though they were heading for Bolougne. However, their true objective was the town of Thérouanne further inland, which they reached on 22 June. They pitched their tents and made ready for a siege. Rhys was one of the chief advisors to the king on the campaign and played an active role as a cavalry 'trouble shooter'. He and his horsemen deterred French probes of the vanguard's position around Thérouanne: '[They] daily scoured the country, and many times encountered with the Frenchmen, and slew and took diverse prisoners, so that the Frenchmen drew not toward the siege, but turned another way.'[3]

On another occasion (27 June), when supplies for the besiegers coming from Guisnes were intercepted by the French force under the command of the Duc de Vendome,

Sir Rhys ap Thomas caused his trumpet to blow to the stirrup, and he with his horsemen sought the Duke of Vendome all the country, which hearing of the coming of Sir Rhys, with great haste retreated back to Blangy Abbey, where the French king's great army lay. Sir Rhys hearing that he was returned came the next day again to the siege.[4]

The king arrived in Calais on 30 June with the bulk of his army, and reached Thérouanne by 1 August. During this march, on 16 July, he was accosted by the French force, 6,000 strong, who appeared on the hill above the town, threatening the English and Welsh forces. This was the signal for one of the daring exploits that made Rhys a legend and provided the poets with a fitting subject for their epics. With just a detachment of pikemen to accompany him, he put the French to flight, capturing four and leaving five dead in the process.

However, there was even greater crisis just a short while later on the night of 26/7 July, which once again saw Rhys at the heart of the action. During that night, two or three of the English guns had been abandoned while a river was being crossed. The next day the king sent Rhys and the Earl of Essex to recover them, along with a detachment of 300 English cavalry, some Burgundian horse and English and German infantry. Rhys managed to retrieve one of the largest guns, but the French were intent on capturing them and attacked in considerable force.

Sir Rhys ap Thomas being a man of great experience, sagely perceived in what case the matter stood, said to the Earl of Essex, sir we be not vii.C. horsemen, let us not be foolish hardy, our commission was to set the gun and none other, let us follow the same, the Earl agreed thereto and so softly and not flying manner retreated and followed the gun.[5]

The French mistook this for flight, but quickly discovered they were wrong when they went in pursuit of the earl and the English forces.

Suddenly appeared in sight a great company of horsemen and the
King knew not what they were: but it was at last perceived that
it was the valiant knight Sir Rhys ap Thomas with his retinue
which came to the King about none: which gently received him
and sent him to the Earl of Essex, which incontinently departed
and encompassed the hill and ran to the Earl and when they
were joined they drew them about the hill accompanied with Sir
Thomas Guildford captain of ii.C archers on horseback to the
tent to have set on the Frenchmen.[6]

The French were forced to retire; Rhys lost one of his own men,
but at least twenty Frenchmen perished.

The main engagement at Thérouanne took place on 16
August. A large French army approached, intending to raise the
siege. The French army was completely routed and chroniclers
christened this the 'Battle of the Spurs'. According to the *Life*,
Rhys captured three prisoners that day including the Duc de
Longeville, only losing two of his own men in the action.[7] Rhys
and the lord steward of Henry VIII's household, the Earl of
Shrewsbury, also secured four French standards. De Longeville
and six other prisoners were consigned to the Tower of London.
Thérouanne was handed over to the English a few days later by
the captain general of the town. The poet Tudur Aled wrote,

It was the raven that routed the hillside of Thérouanne
With his shinning spear and cannon.

The next town to come under attack was Tournai, and the
battle was arranged along similar lines to that of Thérouanne.
The Earl of Shrewsbury was in charge of the vanguard and the

rearguard was under Lord Herbert. The main body of the army was supervised by the king. Rhys was commanded to view one quarter of the town and the Earl of Essex another. They both surveyed the town and then reported back to the king. The city was yielded without a fight by the provost, with a sum of £10,000 sterling for 'the redemption of their laws, customs and liberties.' (*Life*)

When the king and his commanders returned to Calais, Rhys received a reward of 500 marks from Henry himself, perhaps for the capture of de Longeville. Rhys's men arrived back at Calais, ready to be transported to Dover and on to Carew, which had been their original assembly point. The captains that had survived were Sir John Wogan and Sir Owen Perrot from Pembrokeshire, Henry ap John from Carmarthenshire and several of his family.

Such was Rhys's fame when he returned home that the bards sang his praises. Tudur Aled called him 'the envy of England' and he concluded his song with the following lines,

Next after God and the King that day
Rhys and his ravens did bear the sway.[8]

Rhys and his son returned to Wales with even greater influence and undiminished power. The newly created earls (in 1514) of Worcester and Suffolk, Sir Charles Somerset and Charles Brandon, could not prejudice Rhys's hold over South West Wales. In 1515 he was confirmed in his possession of the castle and lordship of Carmarthen and Narberth, and over the next five years was authorised by William Penn, the Steward of Pembroke, to act as steward and receiver of that lordship. The interests of his son Gruffydd were promoted in the lordship of Haverford and Rhos; both Rhys and his son were granted the offices of steward, receiver, approver and chancellor there for life on 16 May 1517. This was done in recognition of their services both at home and abroad. Between the years 1515 and 1519, and possibly at other times, Rhys served as judicial commander in the lordships of Pembroke, Haverford and Cilgerran.

Gruffydd, on his own account, was Mayor of Carmarthen in 1513–14. However, he had already held this office twice previously, in 1504–6 and again in 1511–12. In 1514 he also became Mayor of Kidwelly. Other than that his activities were mainly concerned with the eastern Marches and the English border shires, places with which he was more familiar, from his years of service with Prince Arthur. On 25 September 1514 he was made steward and receiver of the lordship of Dinas, but he was quickly, and perhaps jealously, superseded by Somerset. However, this did not prevent Gruffydd playing a prominent part in maintaining the supervisory role of the Council in the Marches and border shires. Following Henry VIII's accession, the council carried out periodic commissions of the peace, of *oyer* and *terminer*. Also they carried out indentures for good order, which Edward IV and Henry VI had concluded in the past with the Marcher lords and their chief officials.[9] Gruffydd served regularly on such commissions in Gloucestershire, Herefordshire, Shropshire and Worcestershire. These wide-ranging commissions also included Wales and the Marcher lordships, and this enabled commissioners to muster security forces if needed. These forces were supplied by both Gruffydd and his father.

Gruffydd had risen highly in the king's favour. In 1518 he was one of the king's intimate body servants in his household. As such he was nominated for election to the Order of the Garter, a position held at various times by his father; George Talbot, Earl of Shrewsbury; and Thomas Howard, Earl of Surrey. Later in the year he accompanied those who entertained Cardinal Campeggio and his fellow legate from the Pope on their visit to England to discuss an anti-French alliance. Among those attending were Sir Arthur Plantagenet (Edward IVs bastard son), and two Welsh knights, Sir Henry Owen and Sir Gruffydd Dwnn.

Rhys's most important duty in the south-west was to guard the extensive waterways of Milford Sound. Its labyrinthine creeks and rivers wound their way through several of the lordship areas over which both he and his son held sway: Haverford, Rhos, Pembroke and Narberth. The flourishing commercial connections between the ports of South Wales were from time to time threatened by disruption from Ireland. Early in 1520 Rhys was requested by the king to take measures on behalf of the government. In June Henry asked him to send a small contingent of cavalry, about fifty men, to Ireland that August to support the new chief governor Sir Thomas Howard, Earl of Surrey, in supressing a rebellion and asserting royal power.

Meanwhile Rhys had been summoned to court for an important occasion. Both men were requested to travel with Henry to France for a meeting between Henry and the French king, Francis I. The meeting was held in a place called Balinghem, situated between Angers and Guines, and was designed to cement the bond of friendship following the treaty of 1514. Under the guidance of Cardinal Wolsey, the chief European nations were seeking to outlaw war completely among Christian nations. The whole affair lasted two and a half weeks and the place became known as the 'Field of the Cloth of Gold' because of the glamour and extravagance of the meeting.

Henry and Francis were both around the same age; Henry had ruled for eleven years while Francis had been king for just over five, but both were hailed as great Renaissance princes. This was an opportunity for both men to show the wealth and grandeur of their respective courts. Henry and his queen, Catherine, left from Dover around 1 June, Rhys and his wife Dame Jenet also accompanied them in the queen's entourage. The English court had brought with them a temporary palace of timber, which was erected on the site along with tents and pavilions. Hall describes the sight from an eye-witness account:

> Henry and the French King met in a valley called the Golden dale, which lay midway between Guines and Arde where the French King had been staying. In this valley Henry pitched his marquee made of cloth of gold near where a banquet had been prepared. His grace was accompanied by 500 horsemen, and 3,000 foot soldiers and the French King had a similar number of each.
>
> *Life*

The palace covered an area of nearly 12,000 square yards; it contained four blocks with a central courtyard. Each side was 328 feet long. The only solid part was the brick base, roughly 8 feet high. Above the brickwork the 30-feet-high walls were made of cloth or canvas on timber frames, painted to look like stone or brick.

When the two princes met, heralds proclaimed that everyone should stand absolutely still, Henry on one side of the valley,

Francis on the other. They were command to stand there while the two princes rode down the valley; at the bottom they embraced. Henry's sword was held unsheathed by the Marquis of Dorset, while the Duc de Bourbon held Francis's sword.

On 9 June the two kings met at the camp where a tilt yard had been set up, with a green tree with damask leaves nearby. Two shields with the arms of both kings were hung upon the tree, and a proclamation issued that anyone who intended to compete in the tilt, or tourneys, on horseback should bring their shields of arms and have their names entered into the records.

On 11 June Francis came to Guînes to dine with Catherine. He was received by the Duke of Buckingham, the Duke of Suffolk and the Earl of Northumberland among others. All were dressed in cloth of gold, velvet and silks. The evening was spent dancing. At the same time, Henry was in Arde dining with the French queen, with similar surroundings and pastimes. The following day both kings met at the jousts, where Henry was the more successful of the two. These sports continued with a brief interruption on the following day because of a gale.

On 17 June both kings entered the field. Henry's armour skirt and horse trapper were decorated with 2,000 ounces of gold and 1,100 huge pearls. The Earl of Devonshire also entered wearing cloth of gold, tissue cloth and cloth of silver, all elaborately embroidered, and his retinue were dressed similarly.

These and similar entertainments continued until 23 June, when a large and well-appointed chapel was set up in the grounds, decorated with statues of saints and elaborate wall hangings and holy relics, all of which was at Henry's expense. The celebrations concluded the next day, but in retrospect did little to improve relations between the two countries, for in just a couple of months they would once again be at war. The festivities had nearly bankrupted the treasuries of both countries.

Gruffydd had played an important role in the event, taking over from his father on aspects of security. He took a detachment of 100 light cavalry and was commissioned to survey places that might be suitable for ambush, reporting back to the king every morning. Everything went well, and Henry rewarded him with a grey horse, which cost £37 6s 8d, although no doubt Gruffydd's expenses had been a good deal higher. Before the year was out Gruffydd had died, probably from the sweating sickness, or quite possibly from a tournament injury. There was an anonymous epitaph to him written in English, the last lines of which say,

Farewell Cales, and English pales,
Farewell! King Henry, I may not abide,
Death has me lanced into the side.

It may well have been that Gruffydd came to grief during Cardinal Wolsey's mission to Calais between August and November 1521, when he was negotiating a peace between France and the Emperor Charles V, as the 'Cales' referred to in the poem stands for Calais. Gruffydd was buried in Worcester Cathedral close to his master Prince Arthur. The poet responsible for the earlier lines also dwelt upon Gruffydd's interment at Worcester,

To my old master now will I be gone
Prince Arthur still with him to abide,

Yet slaketh my sorrows to think upon,

My chance is to lie so near to his side.

What should I more wish in this world-wide

But in rest perpetual to make merry

With that noble Prince in eternal glory.[10]

Rhys had no other legitimate heir except for his grandson, Rhys ap Gruffydd, who was then fifteen years old. Everything that Rhys had worked for now rested with this young man. There is no record of Rhys's response to this blow, but no doubt he was greatly grieved.

On 5 July 1522 Rhys attended the king for one last time at Greenwich, when Henry was discussing a proposed league with Maximilian and his son, the Archduke Charles. Rhys stayed on at the palace, attending the grand banquet which took place two days later. The meeting was held on the Downs between Dover and Canterbury. Rhys had been summoned to give advice and lend distinction to this diplomatic meeting in which England formed an alliance with Charles. Within a month the emperor had declared war on France, so England naturally had to follow suit. Henry offered to mediate, but that was to no avail. He desperately wanted to restore English lands in France, as well as forming an alliance with Burgundy, and so continued to support Charles. Charles defeated and captured Francis, the French king, at Parva, and set about negotiating terms of peace. Charles did not believe that he owed Henry any favours, so Henry removed his English troops from France, finally signing the Treaty of Mores on 30 August 1525.

Rhys was to take no further part in the future conflicts that arose, and spent his final years attending to his estates and making provision for his grandson and the three ladies of his house, should they outlive him. Rhys had accrued considerable wealth and land, however hardly any documents survive to give a true evaluation of his worth. According to his grandson, Rhys had kept a large hoard of gold and silver coin worth £10,000–£12,000 at his home in Carew. Annuities and fees amounted to well over £400 a year, three-quarters of which had been conferred on him by Henry VII. This gave him the wherewithal to extend his social, landed and administrative influence in South Wales. This amount can only be seen as minimal, because we have no way of knowing about any of his income from military expeditions, royal gifts, marriage negotiations and wardships. Suffice to say that Rhys was as wealthy as a modest English lord.

The majority of Rhys's lands had been inherited from his grandfather and father, and were also considerable. They comprised property scattered throughout the lordship of Kidwelly, the borough of Carmarthenshire and Twyi valley, as well as the lordship of Emlyn Uwch Cuch, which was worth £64 a year, and Narberth, which brought revenues of £125 a year. This enabled Rhys to hold rights as patron in the churches of Llanedin, in the lordship of Kidwelly, Pen-boyr, Llangedr and Cilrehdyn, in the lordship of Emlyn and in the lordship of Narberth, as well as in Llandewi Velfrey, Llanbedr Velfrey, Cilymaenllwyd and Casteldwryan. He had also inherited the Gruffydd family estate in Cardiganshire from his mother, along with the property at Abermarlais in Carmarthenshire. The holdings he had acquired in Gower most probably came with the marriage of his son Gruffydd ap Rhys to Catherine St John.

Rhys was also intent upon securing good marriages for his children, the majority of which were illegitimate. Although he was twice married he only had one legitimate heir, Gruffydd. Three of his mistresses had lived close by in West Wales. One, Gwenllian, was the sister of the Abbot of Talley. In the vicinity of Cardigan Rhys had a relationship with Elizabeth, daughter of Richard Mortimer of Coedmor. Further afield he took Mary Kynaston and Alice Kyffyn as lovers; each woman bore him at least one child. In keeping with his knightly code of chivalry he made settlements for all of his offspring.

Margaret, Gwenllian's eldest daughter, was married to Henry ap John, the Mayor of Carmarthen. They lived at Rhydowen in Llanarthne, where doorways in the house now bear carved shields, one of which is the arms of Rhys ap Thomas. The two sons by this union also fared well: Dafydd the younger married the daughter of John ap Rhys, Mayor of Carmarthen 1498–9; the older Dafydd married Alice, daughter of Arnold Martin of Pembrokeshire. Mary Kynaston's daughter Margaret married Henry ap Thomas Wynot of Orielton; William their son settled in Sandy Haven, not far from Dale; and finally in Cardigan, Jane, daughter of Elizabeth Mortimer, married Dafydd Llewellyn ap Ieuan.

However it was not only his children's marriages that concerned Rhys. He also had a hand in arranging suitable matches for his legitimate grandchildren, the offspring of his son Gruffydd and Catherine St John. Father and son's greatest achievement was to secure Catherine Howard, one of the daughters of Thomas Howard, Earl of Surrey (the Duke of Norfolk from 1514), for Gruffydd's son Rhys ap Gruffydd. This alliance served the interest of both parties, for the growing power and influence of Charles Brandon, Henry VIII's friend and companion in north and north-east Wales, threatened them both.

In 1514 Brandon purchased the wardship of Roger Corbet, who had claim to the lands in Emlyn – these were lands that were occupied by Rhys. The Corbets were related to another of Brandon's friends, Walter Deveraux, Lord Ferrers. In 1513 Brandon had used his influence to secure the wardship of John Carew of Haccombe for his uncle Sir Robert Brandon, and Rhys feared that he might well lose his hold on Carew Castle.

In 1513 the Howards had their own problems with Brandon over military policy and the estate of John, Viscount Lisle, whose wife was one of the daughters of Thomas Howard. The custody of these estates, which were mostly in western counties, were transferred to Brandon from the Howards in 1513 when he was created Viscount Lisle by Henry VIII and was contracted to marry Elizabeth, the child heiress of the Lisles. On 1 February 1513 Brandon was created Duke of Suffolk. The Howards needed allies in the west to counter Brandon's power there, and they certainly found a ready ally in Rhys ap Thomas.

On 12 March 1514 an agreement was made between the duke, Rhys and his son for the marriage of Rhys ap Gruffydd and Catherine Howard. It provided that Rhys ap Gruffydd should marry Catherine by 1521, when he would be fourteen years old. The couple's trustees would receive from Rhys's father and grandfather an estate worth 100 marks, and a further 100 marks would be assigned, but retained, for Rhys ap Thomas to use throughout his lifetime. A similar arrangement was made in Gruffydd's favour.

Rhys also agreed to give his grandson a further 300 marks after the death of himself and his wife and Gruffydd and his wife, and another 100 marks worth of property, which Rhys ap Gruffydd's mother, Catherine St John, presently held in jointure, once she was dead. In return the Duke of Norfolk promised to pay Rhys ap Thomas and his son £200 cash at the time of the marriage and another £200 one year later and a further £200 the year after that. The marriage contract offered other benefits to Rhys ap Thomas because half of the trustees came from East Anglia and the Duke of Norfolk's household, among them Sir Philip Tilney, Sir Robert Wentworth, Sir Thomas Belennerhasset, Sir Nichola Appleyard, Sir Philip Calthorp and Amery Brewer. Such illustrious connections could only benefit Rhys and his family in the long term.

On the Welsh side the trustees were Sir Thomas Cornwall and his son Richard; Sir James ap Owen, a Pembrokeshire knight; William ap John ap Thomas, Rhys's cousin; Dafydd ap Llewelyn ap Gwilym and Gruffydd ap Meureydd Fychan. The unexpected death of Gruffydd ap Rhys in 1521 meant that the marriage needed to be carried out as soon as possible, for Rhys needed desperately to secure the family line. It appears that by 20 August 1522 the marriage had taken place, for when the Duke of Norfolk died at Framlingham Castle in Suffolk on 21 May 1524, Rhys ap Gruffydd was summoned to take his place among the chief mourners who accompanied the funeral procession to Thetford Priory. On 22 June Rhys knelt before the hearse during a solemn dirge in Diss church on the way and at Thetford on 24 June he led the duke's horse into the priory church at the funeral service itself.

Gruffydd also had three daughters and all of them married well; Elizabeth the eldest married Sir Charles Herbert of Troy (Monmouthshire), Mary married John Lutterell, who was heir to the Lutterell estates in Somerset, and the third daughter, whose name is not recorded, married into the White family of Hampshire. Since family connections formed a community, marriage was not seen as a union between two people who loved each other, but a social and political tie to improve the status of the family,[11] and in this respect the family of Rhys ap Thomas fared exceedingly well.

Rhys and his family had acquired the rights and profits from ecclesiastical property, which also added to the coffers. Around the early 1500s Gruffydd had been allowed to lease the considerable Slebech estates of the Knights of St John.[12] The arrangement was not a good one because Gruffydd abused his position by cutting down more than 2,000 oaks without a licence. Furthermore he failed to keep the buildings in good repair, and demanded extortionate sums from the tenants. When payment of the rent fell in arrears, Clement West, the local commander of the order, decided to retaliate, and this resulted in a vicious attack upon his house at Slebech in August 1519. Gruffydd then carried on as usual, undaunted by any remonstrances.

Rhys ap Thomas finally promised to remedy the situation, but it deteriorated further and violence erupted again the following year. West could not appeal to the king, who was at this time in France, so he sent a plea to Cardinal Wolsey in the Court of Requests, but this was to little avail, such was the power and prestige of the Thomas family.

Mortgages were another source of lucrative income. Edmund Carew had mortgaged his estates, which included Carew Castle, to Rhys ap Thomas to help finance his trip to France. It appears that he was shot while sitting in his tent at Thérouanne and so the estates passed to Rhys. On 29 July 1510 Rhys granted a 20-mark mortgage to two tenements at Redberth. Rhys bound himself to the sum of 100 marks to keep the terms of the mortgage. The Flintshire chronicler Elis Gruffydd accused him of unscrupulous acquisition of properties,

> And indeed many regarded his death [the execution of Rhys's grandson in 1531] as Divine retribution for the falsehoods of his ancestors, his grandfather and great grandfather, and for their oppressions and wrongs. They had many a deep curse from the poor people who were neighbours, for depriving them of their houses, lands and riches. For I heard the conversation of folk from that part of the country who said that no common people owned land within twenty miles from the dwelling of old Sir Rhys son of Thomas, that if he desired such lands he would appropriate them without payment or thanks, and the disinherited doubtless cursed him, his children and his grandchildren, which curses in the opinion of many men fell on the family, according to the old proverb which says – the children of Lies are uprooted, and after oppression comes a long death to the oppressors.[13]

Indeed this statement may well have been true, for Rhys augmented the Carew estate by further acquisitions within a radius of 3 miles: Sageston, Yerbeston, Cresselly, Shelston, Pincheston, Milton and Crickchurch. His passion for land and parks knew no bounds. He indulged his passion for hunting and also for cavalry displays. The use of cavalry in warfare had been revived during the Wars of the Roses, as well as the tradition of tournaments and jousts. Acquisition of these lands meant that he could ensure a ready supply of horses and horsemen, and they included patches of land within the estates taken from tenants who were prepared and expected to turn out when needed in his service.

However, Rhys was not necessarily as mercenary as Elis Gruffydd would have us believe, and his loyalty to at least one of his servants is known on record to have extended to manipulation of the mortgage law, which presumably he had also used to his own advantage from time to time.

Wilcock ap Mores Castle was the youngest of Mores Castle's sons, John Wilcock was his youngest son for he after his father's decease had Tretbethod [family home]. He had two sons John and William. This William served Sir Rhys ap Thomas in house. He had Trebethod by the countenance of his master, but his brother John entered into the house and expelled his brother William. Whereon Sir Rhys coming to Llanelli being a great Commander and Chief ruler in those Countries took his man's part and thrust out John Wilcock, threatening the said John that if he would presume to play such a part again he would hang him by the next tree he should find. And, to bridle the said John's attempts, Sir Rhys gave unto his man five pounds in mortgage upon the lands, in presence of the people; but immediately on departure of the people received his money back again. And so the land continued without any rent paid to Sir Rhys or his son, or grandson for their lifetimes.[14]

Up to the time of his departure for France in 1513, Rhys spent a large amount of money on buildings and parklands. He had acquired many properties; Newton House in Dinefwr, the family home, was no longer suitable to accommodate his new position and was left to fall into semi-ruin. His mother's property at Abermarlais in Carmarthenshire fared better, and had a park suitable for hunting, probably at the expense of the peasantry. Leland notes that 'the Park is paled, and encompasses two and a half miles and is well wooded, a well-fortified place, moated, mended and augmented by Sir Rhys ap Thomas'.[15]

Rhys had his defensive and administrative headquarters at Newcastle Emlyn. The castle had few comforts, but contained a large stable block with partitions for twenty-two horses, and a slaughterhouse for the game brought back from hunting expeditions. Rhys also had a smaller castle at Weobley in the Gower, which may have come to him as part of the marriage dowry for his son's wife, Catherine St John, as well as another one in Narberth.

After the death of his son Gruffydd, Rhys spent time assessing the inheritance that would now pass to his grandson. In July and August 1522 lands that Gruffydd held – those worth 100 marks – were finally assigned over to be used by Rhys ap Thomas and his wife Jenet, with the expectation that they would eventually pass to Rhys ap Gruffydd his grandson, who was still a minor. Rhys concluded a thirty-year lease of all the lands settled on Catherine Howard at the time of her marriage in return for 200 marks a year.

Rhys was now in his seventies and he needed to secure all that he had worked for so tirelessly. But the King of the Ravens was fast approaching the end of his life, and little could he have guessed that all he had built would shortly crumble like a house of cards. The *Life* tells us about the last few years of Rhys ap Thomas and his activities.

Rhys having been trained from his earliest youth to the robust exercises of the body now, his age being as our great poet expresses 'a lusty winter' … kept up the spirit of gymnastic discipline in his servants and followers, having set days for a variety of games and pastimes which he would attend in person to encourage and reward.

It seems that even in his declining years he still carried out the pursuits he loved: 'The recreation he most delighted in himself was that of horsemanship, in the knowledge of which he was reputed to excel every man of his time, and in the practice of which he indulged himself with a passion unabated by years.'

Despite his healthy lifestyle, by February 1524 Rhys was failing and made his will. What he was suffering from we do not know, save that when he made his will he was 'syke in body'. Although, according to the *Life*, as his final days approached Rhys was still 'an exemplary temperance in his diet, a methodical distribution of his time, and a discreet husbandage of his vital powers, had secured to Sir Rhys and serenity of mind and it's almost constant concomitant, health of body; nor do I learn that his last days were hurried by any violent or painful disease but was by the favour of heaven suffered to run out gradually and smoothly'.

His last known communication was to the Council in the Marches on behalf of James ap Meureg's sister on the April 4 in Carmarthen. In his will Rhys left substantial legacies to the various ecclesiastical establishments in Wales and beyond with which he had dealings. The Grey Friars in Carmarthen received £20 in cash and £5 in land to establish a perpetual chantry with two priests to pray for the soul of himself and his wife. The Franciscan friars had attracted handsome bequests from Rhys; their house in Hereford, where Henry VIII's great-grandfather Owen Tudor was buried after the battle of Mortimer's Cross in 1461, received a vestment valued at £2 13s 4d. St John's Priory received £6 13s 4d, the record church and St Catherine's hermitage each had a vestment both worth £2 13s 4d. St Peter's church in Carmarthen had a vestment and a chalice worth £5, and St John's and St Barbara's chapels a vestment worth under £2.

Aberystwyth church was given a vestment, as were the churches Llanrhystud and Uwlch Aeron. Llandyfeisant church, near to the family home at Newton in Dinefwr, and the church at Pontargothi, not far from his first wife's home at Cwrt Henri, were also given vestments. Carew received special favours; Dame Jenet was charged with commissioning a silver cross for the parish church and there was no limit to the cost. Rhys did not forget the monastic orders either: he left £8 in cash for a pair of organs for the Cistercian abbey church at Cwm Hir in mid-Wales. The Dominicans at Haverfordwest and Brecon received £2 13s 4d for new vestments.

The remainder of his will dealt with the various bequests to family. Dame Jenet naturally received the lion's share. She received for life almost all of Rhys's holdings in the borough of Carmarthen, £100 cash, a quantity of linen, bedding and all the plate. She was assigned for life the income from one third of his estates, except those lands which he had set aside for the jointure of Catherine Howard, his grandson's wife.

His illegitimate sons, of which he had at least four, received to be divided between them his herds of cattle and sheep. The daughters were not mentioned, and that could well be because they had received benefactions on their various marriages. His heir, Rhys ap Gruffydd, was nominated as his executor with advice and guidance from his maternal grandfather, the Duke of Norfolk, who at this time was also advanced in years. He left one condition, that any remaining plate should be used to negotiate the marriage of young Rhys's sister, who was due to wed Sir Charles Herbert.

His son's widow, Catherine St John, is not mentioned and this is probably because a few months earlier she had married Sir Piers Edgecombe of Cornwall. She had recently left for the family home at Cotehele, taking with her 'all the plate in her keeping which was Gruffydd ap Rhys' and all her stuff of household left by him'.[16]

Rhys died in the summer of 1525 at the Grey Friars in Carmarthen, where he had chosen to take himself several weeks earlier, at the age of seventy-six. The man who had killed the last Plantagenet king of England was laid to rest in the abbey, ironically by the same Franciscan order that had buried Richard III in Leicester. Rhys left instructions that his wife would join him there in due course. The tomb of his mother lay in the friary, as did that of Edmund Tudor, for whom had had been given the commission of erecting a marble tomb by Henry VII. His own tomb was erected on the north side of the choir, close to the high altar. During the Dissolution of the Monasteries not very many years later, his tomb was removed to St Peter's church in Carmarthen and set on the eastern aisle, where it can be seen today.

7

Presumption of the Raven
(1525–1531)

The fortunes of the illustrious family of Rhys ap Thomas now rested on the shoulders of a young man about seventeen years old, Rhys's grandson Rhys ap Gruffydd. He was by all accounts a vigorous and determined young man with high expectations, but after his grandfather's death he found that Henry VIII's regime would offer no continuation of favour to the family. In August 1525 the post of the Supreme Royal Court of Office in South Wales, that of justiciar of the counties of Carmarthenshire and Cardiganshire, was taken over by Walter Devereux, Lord Ferrers, and it was an appointment made for life. Ferrers was also appointed steward and receiver of the lordship of Builth, and constable of its castle, once again for life. These patents were a severe blow to Rhys, but they may have been made because of his youth and lack of experience rather than as a purposeful snub. However, the term for life meant that Rhys was not even seen as being a suitable candidate even when he did reach maturity. Ferrers, on the other hand, was a major landowner in Gloucestershire, Herefordshire and the Marches. This insult was compounded when in on 25 May 1526 Ferrers became Chamberlain of

South Wales, the senior financial office in the southern counties of the principality.

The evidence would suggest that major changes were being undertaken in South Wales as early as 1521, when Gruffydd ap Thomas died. The fact that Sir Rhys by now was in his seventies had also meant that the family hold on these offices was drawing to a close, and now an opportunity presented itself to wrest power out of their hands and place it firmly with Westminster. On 11 December 1521 the rights that Gruffydd ap Thomas had enjoyed as constable of Aberystwyth Castle and as steward, receiver, chancellor and surveyor of the lordship of Haverford were conveyed to Sir William Thomas of Aberglasney. James ap Jankyn, a Yeoman of the Crown, replaced him as constable of the commotes of Cardiganshire on 13 November 1521. Two years before Sir Rhys died, those Welshmen that were recruited to serve in France had also been under the leadership of Lord Ferrers, making Ferrers the most powerful lord in South Wales.

However, there were even more fundamental changes to affect Wales that had been made by Cardinal Wolsey in 1525, possibly in response to the death of Sir Rhys ap Thomas. The commissioners in the Marches were reorganised and a Council of Appeal instated, which was designed to act between the interests of the Welsh and Westminster under the nominal leadership of the nine-year-old Princess Mary. By the end of the year she had been installed at Ludlow. Lord Ferrers was steward of Lady Mary's household and councillor of the Marches.

The new chamberlain was Sir Giles Grenville and by 14 August 1525 he was controller of Mary's household and another one of her councillors. The treasurer of her household was Sir Ralph Egerton, who became steward, receiver, chancellor and surveyor of the lordships of Haverford and Rhos in place of Sir William Thomas. Rhys ap Gruffydd once again was excluded. It would appear that the influence that the Thomas family had once exerted was now no longer going to be tolerated. Gradually the government sought to weaken the political and social dominance exerted in South Wales that had been established by Rhys ap Gruffydd's great-grandfather and grandfather over the last century. However, this created a situation that would give rise to personal resentments and public disorder. The powers of Charles Brandon in the north of Wales were also being curbed at this time, however it bothered him less for he had vested interests elsewhere.

Three of Sir Rhys's personal servants could see how the tide was turning. Thomas Brein, Rhys ap Thomas's clerk; John ap Dafydd ap Rhydderan, a servant; and Lewis ap Thomas ap John, who had been his councillor and one of the executors of his will, quickly transferred their allegiance to Lord Ferrers. Rhys ap Gruffydd charged them with criminally abusing their position while in his grandfather's employment by taking advantage of his grandfather's inability to read or write, thereby robbing him (Rhys ap Gruffydd) of his rightful inheritance. Rhys ap Thomas was not illiterate, so it can only be supposed that the infirmities of old age might have rendered him poor of sight and perhaps arthritic so unable to write. Whatever the truth of the matter, according to Rhys there should have been £10,000–£12,000 in Rhys's coffers, but when his grandfather died only 100 marks were actually found. John ap Dafydd ap Rhydderan was known to have stolen clothes and silks worth 100 marks and all were accused of stealing other items, including blank parchments with the seal of arms of Rhys ap Thomas so that they could issue acquaintances and impose fines for their own enrichment, thereby robbing young Rhys of his inheritance.

Naturally Rhys ap Gruffydd was not happy, and he appealed to Cardinal Wolsey to bring his charge to the Court of Chancery so to avoid the sessions held in South Wales where Lord Ferrers presided. Ferrers protested vigorously, for in 1525 the Council in the Marches had been set up as the Court of Appeal for Wales. Already the stage was set for growing tension between Ferrers and Rhys ap Gruffydd.

It is not clear what the relationship was between Rhys ap Gruffydd and Cardinal Wolsey. In 1529 he reminds Wolsey about the loyal service that he given him, in return no doubt for lenient treatment at the cardinal's hands. He may well have been introduced to the cardinal by the Howards. There is one piece of written information that may shed some light on Rhys's contacts with the cardinal. When Wolsey went to Calais in 1527 to meet with Francis, the French king, Rhys was in the entourage along with his uncle, Sir John St John.

Wolsey's biographer and usher wrote that Wolsey treated Rhys with good-humoured familiarity. He also wrote that while instructing his entourage to act as befitted servants of Henry VIII, he reminded them that the French king's retinue

will be at the first meeting as familiar with you as they had been acquainted with you long before and common with you in the French tongue as though you understand every word they spoke; therefore in like manner, and you be familiar with them again as they be with you; if they speak to you in the French tongue then you speak to them in the English tongue for if you understand not them, they shall no more understand you. And my lord speaking merely to one of all the gentlemen there (being a Welshman) said Rhys; said he, speak you Welsh to him. And I am well assured that your Welsh shall be more defuse to him, than his French shall be to you.[1]

However, the tension between Ferrers and Rhys was mounting and as Ferrers did not call upon his services to fill any of the available positions, preferring to employ border gentry, Rhys's animosity grew. Rhys's wife, Catherine Howard, saw this as sinister because Ferrers would and could claim protection of the law, whether or not he was in the right. This hostility was becoming a well-known fact. On 30 June 1528 Rhys and two of his servants, Hugh and William Mores, were attacked while they were on their way to London. No doubt this attack was on the orders of Ferrers. They were detained in Oxford Castle by the sheriff, but they appealed to Wolsey and were eventually released. Meanwhile, Sir John Vessey, the Bishop of Exeter and President of Princess Mary's Council in the Marches, reported on 5 July 1528 that the 'matter between Lord Ferrers and young Mr Rhys is pacified'. Fuel was added to the fire when on 12 December the king authorised Ferrers and Rhys to enlist cohorts of retainers beyond what the law allowed. Both sides could now call upon large retinues of men should hostilities ensue.

By February Rhys once again petitioned Wolsey, this time asking to be appointed Deputy Justiciar and Deputy Chamberlain of South Wales, one again going over the head of Ferrers, to whom Rhys promised to pay whatever sum Wolsey considered appropriate. At the same time he denounced Ferrers' deputies for oppressing his servants and tenants. Rhys, however, did not get the appointments he wished.

The chronicler Elis Gruffydd, who disliked the family of Rhys ap Thomas, said that Ferrers was in fact jealous of Rhys's popularity: 'When Rhys went to Wales the whole country turned out to welcome him, and this made Lord Ferrers envious and jealous.'[2] It seems plausible that this may well have been the case, but Wolsey viewed it merely as a breakdown in personal relationships. Nevertheless by 1529 they were at each other's throats again.

Rhys's actions in South Wales, using what little authority he had there, did not mirror those of his illustrious grandfather. In Pembrokeshire he acted as steward and receiver on behalf of Sir William Parr, but he showed a certain high-handedness in his dealings. In early 1528 there was a major invasion of south Pembrokeshire by Irishmen from the territories of the Irish rebel James Fitz Maurice, the Earl of Desmond. He had been in intrigue with France and the emperor. Rhys responded to this insurgence with deportations and exclusions, which were authorised from Pembroke Castle in the absence of Sir William Parr. The local mayor and burgess of Tenby complained and actually resisted the order, so Rhys appealed to Wolsey to grant him the extra powers he required to prevent the Pembrokeshire gentry from harbouring Irishmen and taking them into their service.

However, what was even more to his detriment was an incident that took place in the spring of 1529. According to the merchants of Tenby, freebooters were operating from a Bristol ship off the coast of Pembrokeshire and were deterring the Portuguese and Breton merchants from trading with the towns.

Meanwhile, the pirates entered Milford Haven with a cargo of salt for sale, but Rhys was unable to persuade the captain to answer the complaints that had been made against him in the king's court. The locals wanted to seize the ship in response, but Rhys was not willing to do this. Instead he agreed to the merchant's suggestion that he should buy the salt ship with the 30 tons of salt it carried, arm it and use it against the freebooters, who in the meantime had seized and robbed another Bristol ship bound for Ireland.

Rhys offered to take the side of the captain, William Hughes, before the king and Wolsey, and managed to persuade him to take charge of the salt ship, which Rhys had armed with twelve canon and 200 men, along with another vessel, the *Matthew*, and three large coastal barges, in order to apprehend the freebooters.

The freebooters continued with their activities, even pursuing ten picards[3] from Ireland into Milford Sound. Rhys's fleet attempted to surround the freebooters' ship in order to delay their departure, but as the vessel tried to leave the sound, Rhys's men assembled on both sides of the Haven, the wind dropped and the ship hit a rock, leaving the freebooters with no alternative but to surrender. Rhys quickly despatched them to Pembroke Castle and claimed half the value of the ship and its tackle as prize, and requested of Wolsey to keep the vessel to be used in defence of the coast. Rhys was ordered to try the captain and the pirates for felony, so he sent them to Pembroke Castle.

On 10 July the possible owner of the salt ship, John Salman from Southampton, was the chief appellant; the defendants were William Hughes and his men and they were found guilty, but kept in prison pending the finding of sureties for good behaviour. Each jury member was obligated for a sum of £100 to provide further evidence if needed. The whole business was less than fair to Salman, and unjust toward the pirates, however Rhys ap Gruffydd had profited from the incident while posing as a guardian of the king's coast.

Later in 1529 further questionable actions were undertaken by Rhys. A Spanish ship called the *Mary*, out of Bilbao, put into the port at Tenby to trade. An armed galleon captained by Nicholas Quayle of Morlaix in Brittany arrived at the same time, and claimed that the *Mary* originally had belonged to him and John Legett, and had been wrongfully captured by the emperor in peace time.

The Spanish captain, Melchior de Loriaga, denied this, saying that the vessel had been taken off the Île de Ré in mid-February 1528 after war had been declared between the emperor and the French king, and was therefore legally Spanish. Melchior sought aid from the Chancellor of England, Sir Thomas More, to have the ship restored, along with tackle and ordinance worth about £100, which had been taken to Carmarthen. Rhys ap Gruffydd intervened in collusion with Quayle. He announced that he would be Judge of the Admiralty and ordered the arrest of the *Mary*, which he then purchased from Quayle. He expelled the Spanish sailors, and prepared the vessel for sea, armed with men and artillery to deploy it on freebooting missions out of Milford Haven.

Loriaga was forced to house himself and his men in Tenby at his own expense for two months before suitable transportation could be found to return them home, because Rhys had forbidden their earlier departure. At the court in Tenby, the mayor bound Quayle and his companions to prove by 24 June that he was the owner of the ship, and to provide his version

of events, otherwise he was to compensate Loriaga. However, Quayle and his companions fled to Brittany, while the mayor was being intimidated by Rhys until he let the matter drop.

Such behaviour was less than satisfactory from a descendent of the illustrious Rhys ap Thomas, and no doubt Rhys was aware that the government was displeased by his manipulation of the law. In order to redeem himself, on 20 January 1529 he reported to Wolsey from his home in Carew on an incident that he hoped would enhance his standing at court. It appears that he apprehended a man called John Sant, who in 1528 had killed a servant of Sir William Brereton, a Cheshire gentleman who was a member of the king's privy chamber. Sant had been responsible for spreading rumours around Ludlow, where the Council in the Marches usually met, that Henry VIII was dead. Sant was arrested in the lordship of Lord Audley, possibly at Llandovery, and confined in a castle close by, from which he escaped. Rhys, however, recaptured him and believed that this act would restore his prestige.

Nevertheless, the problems that he had caused in South Wales were more damaging to his reputation. There had been complaints about him lodged in the Chancery, the court in the Marches and the Star Chamber, and further trouble was about to erupt. In June 1529 the Great Sessions were to be held in Carmarthen and presided over by Lord Ferrers. Ferrers had authorised his lieutenant James Leche, who was bailiff of the borough, to request lodgings from the mayor for himself and his entourage. The mayor naturally authorised his sergeants to assign certain houses to Ferrers' servants. Rhys ap Gruffydd was determined to show a force of strength at the sessions, so 'upon a wilful mind and maliciously disposed to make quarrel', made similar arrangements to lodge his servants in the town. When Leche arrived, most of the available accommodation had been taken by Rhys's men. Thomas ap Morgan had fixed Rhys's badges, painted on paper, to the doors of the houses that had been assigned to Ferrers' men to prevent them from lodging there.

Rhys's wife, Catherine, gave a different version of events, saying that Ferrers' men had removed the badges and appropriated the lodgings meant for her husband's entourage. On 6 June Rhys called on his friends and kinsmen in Carmarthenshire and Cardiganshire. He made proclamations in the county churches telling them to come armed to Carmarthen the next day. Dafydd ap Rhys Baas, a bastard son of Rhys ap Thomas, later admitted issuing proclamations in the churches at Llansadwrn and Llanwrda, and the curate of Ucurda also admitted his involvement. The outcome remains a mystery, but what is evident is that there was a dangerous threat to public order, and as it was left unresolved this would later erupt into a more serious incident.

This incident took place a week later at Carmarthen Castle. Two of Rhys's servants and his kinsman Thomas ap Owain, the king's attorney in the lordship of Haverford, were arrested by Ferrers for having taken part in the earlier violence and put into prison in the castle. Thomas had to pay 650 marks to ensure his peaceful behaviour. Later in the evening of 15 June, around 7 p.m., Rhys and forty well-armed men burst into the castle and headed for Ferrers' chamber, where he was in conference. An argument concerning the arrest of Thomas ensued, and Rhys and Ferrers drew their daggers and threatened each other. Ferrers sent his chamberlain to report the incident to Wolsey that evening, and to the president of the Council in the Marches the following day.

Ferrers said that his men had disarmed Rhys and that he was now being held in custody without bail under a bond of £1,000. One of the men present, formerly one of Rhys ap Thomas's entourage, Lewis ap Thomas ap John, was wounded in the head during the skirmish.

Once again Catherine came to the aid of her husband, writing immediately to Wolsey and telling him that Rhys had been wounded in the arm and that Thomas ap Owain had been wrongfully arrested for trying to release another of Rhys's servants, Jankyn, from the castle. She warned Wolsey of the disastrous effects these actions would have locally and played upon the fact that she was the half-sister of the Duke of Norfolk. She then applied herself to assembling more of Rhys's friends and acquaintances in Carmarthenshire, Cardiganshire and Pembrokeshire as well as the country estates in order to rescue Rhys.

That night roughly 140 men penetrated the outskirts of Carmarthen, making their way to Dark Gate. They sent messages to Ferrers ordering him to release Rhys, or to at least refrain from sending him to Westminster – if he refused they would burn the castle and release Rhys themselves. The following day more insurgents arrived to give added weight to the rebellion. These were not just any men, but notable men of the county including Rhys Rede of Carmarthenshire and Lewis ap Hywel ap Philip. Several of the ringleaders from Pembrokeshire had had close links to Rhys ap Thomas, for example John Wogan and William ap Owain, who had both presided at the Pembrokeshire county court in 1526 in place of Rhys.

161

Rhys and 120 of the ringleaders were indicted as rebels in the county court at Carmarthen and the affair was reported to the Star Chamber. Ferrers exaggerated the situation: 'The great rebel and insurrection of the people … there was not such an insurrection in Wales at any time that a man can remember.'[4] Rhys was placed under a bond of £1,000 to keep the peace and remain in Carmarthen Castle until instructions arrived from the Council in the Marches. However, until the issues could be resolved and Rhys and Ferrers reproved, the situation was not going to change. This was evident later in the year, on 6 August prior to the hearing in the Star Chamber, when two of Rhys's servants – Gruffydd ap Morgan, his usher, and Gruffydd ap John, his falconer – ambushed and killed Ferrers' lieutenant and justiciar, Reynold ap Morgan. It was later reported that these two men were seen shortly after the deed, in Tenby, in the company of Rhys.

Meanwhile, on the very day that Carmarthen was in turmoil, a special court was convened at Blackfriars to pass judgement on the king's marriage. For some time Henry had been trying to procure an annulment of his marriage to Catherine of Aragon in order to marry Anne Boleyn. This had brought him into conflict with Catherine's nephew Charles V and the Pope, who refused to grant Henry his annulment.

Finally the king took action and ordered both men to lay their charges against each other at the Council in the Marches as the designated court of appeal for Wales. Rhys and Ferrers appeared before the tribunal, but the chronicler Elis Gruffydd was not impressed:

And it chanced that I was present on that day with many others from all parts of the kingdom, when and where I heard the ugliest accusations and charges that the two gentlemen could bring against each other – charges and accusations which thousands of poor men would not for any amount of wealth have had brought against them by word of mouth, much less in writing ... and notwithstanding the numerous threats of the Cardinal against them I never once heard a word from him in defence of the poor whom both had grievously wronged according to the written statements of each about the other ... each of them made the most serious complaints and allegations against the other that was possible, not only about the affray that had been between them, but in respect of the oppression of the people and the bribery of which each was said the other was guilty. And when the court had listened to their mutual accusations for some time, the Cardinal summoned the case before him into the Star Chamber.[5]

Both men were bound in an obligation bond of £1,000 to keep the peace until Michaelmas time, when the matter would be heard in the Star Chamber at Westminster. They were both censured for their behaviour and told by Wolsey to go about their lawful business in peace. However this proved to be no solution to the problem. Rhys had shown little regard or respect for the king's authority or the king's justiciar and Ferrers had not displayed any discretion in his handling of Rhys or with the situations that had arisen.

By the beginning of October 1529 Wolsey was suddenly and dramatically removed from office. He had been trying to procure papal dispensation for the annulment of Henry's marriage to Catherine of Aragon so the king could remarry. The business was slow and laborious and Henry had grown tired of waiting and he believed that Wolsey was not working hard enough to procure the Pope's approval. In 1529 Wolsey was arrested and stripped of all his offices and property. Wolsey retreated to York, but no sooner had he arrived there than he was accused of treason by the Duke of Northumberland and despatched back to London for trial. Fortunately for Wolsey, he was taken ill on the return journey and died on 29 November 1530 in Leicester.

Several months after the incident in the Star Chamber, Catherine Howard once again took up her husband's cause regarding the assault on his position in Pembrokeshire, where he held William Parr's commission as steward and receiver. Rhys's behaviour in Tenby had led to petitions being lodged in the Chancery during 1529–30. Thomas More, who had replaced Wolsey, now intervened and on 22 June William Parr's offices were reaffirmed, leaving Rhys's compact with Parr seemingly at an end. Catherine Howard laid siege to Ferrers and some of his men were killed. This may have happened around the same time that James ap Gruffydd ap Hywel installed himself in Rhys's castle at Newcastle Emlyn with a strong force. James was a son of Rhys ap Thomas's sister Sage, who lived at Castell Maelgwyn, near Cilgerran. An attempt to arrest him following the issue of a royal warrant by Ferrers resulted in the wounding of William Vaughan of Cilgerran, another adherent of Rhys ap Thomas. Finally James Leche apprehended him, and he was sent to the Tower of London.

On 15 October Rhys ap Gruffydd was arrested, no doubt on the king's orders, for he was becoming a great embarrassment to Henry, especially as his behaviour as well as his kinship reflected on Henry's attempts to procure his annulment. The

Imperial ambassador, Eustace Chapuys, was told that 'he himself has threatened to finish what his wife had begun'.[6] Rhys was committed to the Tower, but he was released in June 1531 because of ill health. His standing with the government and the king had been immeasurably damaged, but before long other factors would finally cast Rhys into the abyss.

On 21 October, just three months after his release, he was re-arrested, and on the 26 October Chapuys reported that Rhys planned to escape to Scotland or to the Imperial court to plot against the king. Rhys's trial before the King's Bench took place on 22 November on an indictment of treason; he was framed by a Middlesex jury of presentment, which was most probably officially inspired. The charges arose from events that had taken place in London, so the case could not be heard by the Council in the Marches. They had gathered information about recent plots in the capital from Rhys's steward, William Wolf, and one of his chaplains from Haverford, who had been summoned to the Star Chamber; however, Thomas Cranmer discharged the chaplain from appearing.

It was alleged that on the 28 August 1531, at Rhys's lodgings in Islington, he and William Hughes from Carew plotted the deposition and death of Henry VIII. The old prophecies were resurrected that implicated James V of Scotland; they inferred that he, along with the Red Hand and the Raven, would conquer England. The raven in this case did not necessarily refer to Rhys, but one of his forebears, Owain Llangoch (d. 1378), the elusive Welsh rebel who was the last direct descendent of the Welsh princes of Gwynedd. It was unfortunate that Rhys's badge bore the symbol of three ravens. These prophecies, centuries old, that saw attacks on England and its king from the north, west,

Wales, Ireland and Scotland gained currency from time to time, and the paranoia of Henry VIII about his security as king had no doubt given rise to their resurgence.

It was also alleged that Rhys tried to raise £2,000 by mortgaging his lands, notably in the lordships of Narberth and Carew, to Robert White, a London clothier, in order for him to make his way to the Isle of Man and Ireland on his way to Scotland, where King James was expected to lead an army against England and would install Rhys in the principality of Wales.

On 1 September Rhys sent one of his men, Edward Llwyd, to the Tower to persuade his kinsman James ap Gruffydd ap Hywel to join in the plot. Llwyd told him that if William Hughes came he would give him credence as well, and there followed a series of messages passing to and fro between the Tower and Rhys. On the third of the month James negotiated on Rhys's behalf with one of his creditors, a London merchant called John Hughes, to raise money by selling or mortgaging land, which would pay off James's debts and acquire a considerable sum of cash.

The next day, William Hughes entered the Tower with a priest whose remit was to seal the arrangements by administering the sacrament to James. According to Justice Spelman's notes James refused the sacraments, but agreed to the rest of the plan. Two incidents took place during the period 4–21 September. First James escaped from the Tower and sought sanctuary at Westminster Abbey, and second Rhys was re-arrested and placed in the Tower.

Chapuys, in his correspondence to his emperor Charles V, gives a great deal of inside information as to what was taking place at this time, and his documents also shed a good deal of light upon what happened to Rhys. Charles was nephew to Catherine of Aragon and at this time Henry was seeking a divorce from her, hoping to instate Anne Boleyn in her place, so naturally Charles was anxious about his aunt. Henry on the other hand was increasingly concerned about the failure of Catherine to produce an heir, and he had become highly suspicious of anyone who might have a claim on the throne. In 1521 the Duke of Buckingham had been executed after an alleged plot to kill the king. Rhys also had connections that may have worried Henry; apart from his own Welsh heritage he was linked to the king through his mother, Catherine St John, who incidentally was the aunt of Anne Boleyn. One of the charges against Rhys in 1531 was that he had adopted the name Fitz Urien, which had venerable associations with the British kings of Rheged. However, other members of his family had done so previously, as far back as the fourteenth century and Elidir Ddu.

Rhys was found guilty of treason, and on 4 December 1531 he was taken to Tower Hill and executed. William Hughes was taken to Tyburn the same day and was hanged, drawn and quartered. No doubt Ferrers and other members of the Council in the Marches were delighted with the result. Rhys's body was interred in the Holy Cross Friary, just a short distance from his place of execution. Chapuys noted the similarities between the trial of Buckingham and that of Rhys and the implications of their heritage in prompting a death sentence, even commenting on the fact that they had both been executed on the same spot. It was also noted by Chapuys that at the time of Rhys's execution he and his wife were accused of speaking disparagingly of Anne Boleyn, and she had exerted influence to have Rhys condemned: 'There is a rumour about town that had it not been for the Lady, who hated him because he and his wife had spoken disparagingly of her, he would have been pardoned and escaped his miserable fate.'[7]

There was a story circulating in the seventeenth century related by Henry Rice (a descendant of Rhys ap Thomas) that he had heard from Charles Howard, Earl of Norfolk (d. 1625). The tradition goes that one day the king was out hawking at Wandsworth when his falcon seized a fowl, but a raven swooped down and took the fowl from the falcon. One of the king's companions remarked on the presumption of the raven, which 'deserved to be pulled down from its perch to secure your majesty'. True or not, this story gives us some idea of what people perceived to be Henry's anxieties about Rhys ap Gruffydd.

Rhys's trial had been a farce. His fate seemed harsh considering his pedigree, as Chapuys states, '[Rhys's] father was formerly Governor of Wales, as was his grandfather also and one of those who did great service to Henry VII in his early necessities and the conquest of this kingdom.'[8]

Not everyone believed that the treatment this prominent Welshman received would bode well for Anglo-Welsh relations in the future. One such man was John Hale, the Vicar of Isleworth, who in May 1534 gave this opinion: 'I think not contrary but they [the Welsh] will join and take part with Irish, and so invade our realm. If they do so, doubt ye not that they shall have aid and strength enough in England.'[9]

Although the young Rhys had not been an inspiring leader like his grandfather, his execution, like that of Buckingham ten years earlier, was, as Griffiths says, 'no more than an act of judicial murder based on charges devised to suit the prevailing political and dynastic situation'.[10] Not only was Rhys a troublesome relative of the king, but his Howard kinsmen may also have needed bringing to heel.

Griffith explains that the charges of treason may be connected with the proposals made in 1531 by Thomas Cromwell and his and Anne Boleyn's ally, Thomas Audley, Speaker of the Commons, to extend the treason laws in order to take account of opposition that might come from Henry VIII's treatment of Queen Catherine, the clergy and the Pope. In 1531 the king instructed Cromwell to insert a clause in the proposed bill to the effect that 'the first accused of any manner treason shall have his pardon and a certain sum for his labour for the detection of any such treason'. This provision would have been an inducement to Edward Llwyd and James ap Gruffydd ap Hywel to turn on Rhys.

Another of the proposals inserted was that it would be considered treason to 'consent or agree, privily or openly, to contribute or pay any sums of money to any foreign prince or other estate, contrary to the prerogative royal or in prejudice to the king's business and this his business'. This may have had a bearing on Rhys's execution in 1531, for the bill appears to have been abandoned soon afterwards and was never presented to Parliament in 1532. Had this merely been concocted in order to do away with Rhys, and abandoned once that was accomplished?

The chief architect of Rhys's trial and execution had been Thomas Cromwell, although he wasn't actually named in any of the relating documents. The patronage and influence that was made available in Wales after Rhys's attainder may explain why it was Cromwell who kept Rhys's family archives in his possession. Cromwell was fast becoming the pre-eminent advisor of Henry VIII. The Duke of Norfolk (Howard), who had dominated the king's council earlier in the year, had no reason to encourage Cromwell's fortunes: Rhys's attainder killed two birds with one stone as far as Cromwell was concerned.

Rhys ap Gruffydd was a victim of his time and Griffiths sums this up well when he says he was 'a victim of dynastic circumstances beyond his control, of personal relationships and political rivalries of the most intense sort, and of developments, that in retrospect made him one of the earliest martyrs of the English Reformation'.[11] Perhaps this may have gone some way to recalling the reputation of the great Rhys ap Thomas, but the remainder of the family would have to fight long and hard for recognition and reinstatement of their rights.

8

Resurrection
(1547–2013)

The quest to reinstate the family's reputation and restore their lands began soon after Henry VIII's death in 1547. This would not be an easy task for Gruffydd ap Rhys, Rhys's son. According to the Act of Attainder in 1531, the lands and properties of Rhys ap Gruffydd were forfeited to the Crown, however, the act safeguarded the interests of the three widows of the family with regard to land and possessions, which they held for life.

In 1536 half the estates were held by Dame Jenet (d. 1535), Dame Catherine (d. 1553) and Lady Catherine Howard (d. 1544), who had quickly remarried Henry, Lord Daubney, after Rhys's execution. Between them they enjoyed an annual income of roughly £360. Dame Jenet's property was mostly in Carmarthen and Dame Catherine's in Gower, while Lady Catherine's estates in Pembrokeshire, especially the Carew estate, made her the wealthiest of the three. The remainder of Rhys's fortunes went to the Crown, and they leased the majority of these properties to various families of note; all of these leases were under the administration of Thomas Cromwell.

After Rhys was executed, his two sons, Thomas and Gruffydd, were placed in the charge of the Bishop of Durham,

Cuthbert Tunstall. This meant that the children were safely out of the way in the North, and could pose no threat to the crown. It is possible that while they were there they may have had some contact with their Howard relatives. When Thomas was seventeen he escaped over the border to Scotland, where he went into the service of the infant Mary, Queen of Scots. Thomas was apparently given 200 men at the time of the insurrection of Donald Dubh, who had the support of the highlanders in his bid to become Lord of the Isles. Following an ambush of Queen Mary's army at Kinlochlochy in July 1544, Thomas was killed.

It was left to Gruffydd to try to get the family's name and lands reinstated. He presented a petition on behalf of the family at the first parliament of Edward VI. He asked for the stain of treason to be removed from the family name, but acknowledged that the Crown held rights over his land. He was granted his request to remove the stain of treason, but nothing else was forthcoming. The reign of Queen Mary offered slightly more promise, mainly because Rhys had sided with her mother, Catherine of Aragon, and Catherine's other ally, the Duke of Norfolk, had just recently been restored to his estates and titles in August 1553.

On 10 October 1554 Gruffydd was granted the manors of Angle and Burton in south Pembrokeshire, whose annual value was £65 19s 5d, and in 1555 was he given the lordship and castle of Carew. The tide seemed to be turning in his favour, but the family's lingering ill fortune was about to strike Gruffydd. While he was on a visit to Auckland in County Durham, to visit the home of Tunstall, he was involved in a murder.

On 30 September 1557 at 8 o'clock in the evening, Matthew Walshe was on his way home when he was waylaid and killed by his wife Agnes, Gruffydd and a tailor called James Halle, who was Gruffydd's servant. There is no evidence to indicate what had prompted this act, but Bishop Tunstall declared that it was 'a shameful murder'. Gruffydd and his accomplices fled to Wales and on 10 October Gruffydd's lands were seized by the Council in the Marches. Soon afterwards the murderers were apprehended, which led to attainder for Gruffydd, forfeiting all the properties that he had only just accumulated. This was a catastrophe for the family fortunes.

Grants from the estates were now made to others, for example Thomas Heyborne, a Yeoman of the Guard, received lands at St Florence (Pembs.) for life. Thomas Borage received the manor at Angle, while Catherine's estates of Weobley and Gower went in 1560 to the Earl of Pembroke. By the time of Mary's death, Gruffydd's fortunes were at their lowest ebb, and he could not expect a great deal of sympathy from her successor, Elizabeth I. What he desperately needed was to first gain a pardon for his crime.

During this period he had married Elinor, the daughter of Sir Thomas Jones, a man who controlled a number of Rhys ap Gruffydd's estates. When he died not long after the marriage had taken place, it was Elinor among others who managed to secure him a pardon. Gruffydd wanted to play a public role in Carmarthenshire and so he persisted with his petitions to the queen until she relented. On 13 January 1560 she approved arrangements for Gruffydd to recover a great proportion of his mother's estates in south Pembrokeshire, with the exception of Carew. In total the lands he received yielded about £100 a year. However he was not so lucky regarding his grandmother's lands in Gower, all of which were given to William Herbert,

Earl of Pembroke. Gruffydd also requested the restoration of all his father's lands that were still held by the Crown, but this was to little avail.

Elizabeth had nominated him a JP in Carmarthen from 1564 and he was sheriff of the county from 1567 to 1583. She also began to restore to him some of his father's lands at this time, but only on a lease basis. Gruffydd tried a different route to petitioning the queen by going through the Earl of Sussex. Sussex, like Gruffydd, had a mother who was one of the Howard daughters, so they had a filial connection. Likewise their great-grandfathers had played an instrumental role in Henry VII's founding of the Tudor dynasty, and therefore had a stake in its future. Gruffydd went even further and in a public document characterised his attained father as the dupe of evil men.

> That whereas Sir Rhys ap Thomas, Knight, great grandfather unto your said servant did in his life time many great and acceptable services to your Majesty's most noble grandfather and father of worthy memories, especially with the service of 1800 horsemen at his own charge at the landing of your Majesty's grandfather at Milford Haven in Wales and at the battle of Bosworth. And afterward with 1500 horsemen at Blackheath field where he took the Lord Audley prisoner and since the service of your most noble father at Tournai and Therouanne with the 15000 horses where he also took prisoner the Duc Longeville. In recompense of which and other his many true and faithful services it pleased their Majesties graciously to advance him to the most noble order of the Garter and to other great offices and livings in south Wales where he then dwelled. After his death Rhys Gruffydd

Esquire, heir to the said Sir Rhys and father to your majesty's said servant, being a young gentleman of good hope and like credit was persuaded by one James Griffith ap Howel his near kinsman (who was corrupted by the said adversaries of Rhys Gruffydd) to put his hand to a blank wherein the said James secured such matters to be written as contained treason, as he the said James being fled out of the realm for diverse treasons and accepted in such diverse pardons, afterward confessed, for which the said Rhys Gruffydd was attained, whereby all his living amounting to the yearly value of a thousand pounds at the least came to the hands of your most noble father.[1]

Gruffydd requested that if his lands could not be returned then he would lease them, but nothing was forthcoming and on 1 September 1592 he died.

His son Walter, who was in the queen's service, carried on with his father's efforts and began his quest in the Court of Wards, which started an enquiry into Rhys's estate in February 1594. Angle and Burton manors were returned to the family, along with Newton in Pembrokeshire and some other lands in Carmarthenshire and Cardiganshire that were on lease. The other petitions made to Elizabeth were still to no avail. In March 1603, Walter was knighted by the new king, James, and on 30 May 1604 he was elected to serve in James's first parliament.

Once again in 1623 he petitioned the king to restore the lands held by the Crown, and once again this was not forthcoming. By the time that Charles I succeeded, practically all the lands belonging to the family had been disposed of and it was useless to try and regain them. However, Walter's son Henry achieved some measure of honour for the family name by being appointed to the Privy Chamber.

Henry Rice, as he was now known, had taken a degree at Oxford in 1607, where he was in contact with humanist studies, and this prompted him to compose a history of his family. The *Life of Sir Rhys ap Thomas and the Objections to the Charges against Rhys ap Gruffydd* was a mixture of family tradition and antiquarian research, with the primary aim of restoring the reputation and material fortune of the 'Rices of Newton'. *The Life of Sir Rhys ap Thomas* was first published in its entirety in 1796 in the inaugural volume of the *Cambrian Register* and did not appear again in print until 1993.[2] It is an invaluable piece of work for understanding the life and times of this remarkable Welshman who helped shape the course of history; as Griffiths says of the work, 'seldom has a family in such dire straits been so well served by the intellectual accomplishments of the English and Welsh Renaissance.'[3]

In 1983, archaeological rescue work was undertaken at the site of the Grey Friars in Carmarthen, the original resting place of Sir Rhys ap Thomas, in advance of the building of a new Tesco store.[4] During the excavations a fragment of burnt, leaded stained-glass window was unearthed and was taken to the Department of Archaeology in Cardiff for conservation. The small fragment of glass was found to depict a raven, the arms of Rhys ap Thomas, and the leaded fragment was dated to the initial founding of the friary in the thirteenth century. This made the fragment the oldest piece of leaded window still surviving in the whole of Britain. The glass itself proved to be more difficult to date, but appeared to have been in place by the time of Gruffydd ap Nicholas and was no doubt indicative of the family's patronage of the friary.

Once again the 'ravens of Dinefwr' were making news, albeit local. Rhys ap Thomas's name was resurrected and two years later, on the 500th anniversary of Bosworth Field, the role played by Rhys and the Welsh in securing victory for Henry Tudor was acted out throughout Wales. Many visitors to South Wales that summer were introduced to this little-known Welsh 'king'. A BBC Radio 4 play, *The Echo of the Dragon*, was commissioned for the event, which depicted Rhys's final remorse over killing Richard as he lay dying at the Grey Friars.[4] Another thirty years have passed and Rhys's memory has faded yet again, however a further resurrection has taken place that once again brings Sir Rhys ap Thomas to the fore.

In a Leicestershire car park the body of King Richard III, the 'king in the car park', as he has now been designated, was discovered where it had been buried at the site of the Grey Friars church. The ensuing media coverage has been overwhelming and all the old arguments about this most controversial of English monarchs have also been resurrected. Richard's bones have yielded a great deal of information, so that we may obtain a truer picture of the last of the Plantagenet monarchs, but they cannot answer other intriguing questions about his reign or his character; these will possibly always remain an enigma. One of the most important pieces of information gleaned from the analysis was that the blow that actually killed him was made by a hand axe, a halberd, the favourite weapon of Rhys ap Thomas. It would appear that Guto'r Glyn was correct when he attributed that blow to Rhys.

Richard's reputation and appearance was manufactured by William Shakespeare in his play *Richard III*, and consequently made him perhaps the most well-known monarch for all the wrong reasons. Had Philip Henslowe's play *Henry of Richmond Part Two* survived, in which Rhys ap Thomas played a leading role, then perhaps we would have also become more familiar with this Welshman.[5] Now it would seem to be a fitting moment for both these men to be brought into the public eye for the last time. They were both victims of the times into which they were born, both subjected to the factionalised loyalties of that bloody period of English history, and both ended their days with the Grey Friars.

Rhys was not a traitor, but he most probably realised that if a Welshman could be placed on the throne then the principality might benefit more than it had done under English rule. It was a chance he took when he declared for Henry, and he would have been all too aware of the consequences of failure. Rhys was fighting for his life and that of his countrymen. His act was not premeditated, his blow to the king was one of many that day, *but* it was the fatal blow. The blow that would earn him the epithet of 'the man who killed Richard III', and serve to resurrect his story once again.

Newport Community
Learning & Libraries

Acknowledgements

No work is the sole endeavour of the author alone and this work is no exception. Without the excellent research of Ralph Griffiths in his book *Sir Rhys ap Thomas and his Family* then there would be many gaps in our knowledge of Sir Rhys, and I am greatly indebted to this work.

I would like to thank Bosworth Battlefield Heritage Site for permission to use photographs of the Rhys ap Thomas's horse harness badge and halberd. I offer special thanks to Dr Patricia Taylor for some of the Carmarthenshire photographs, which she kindly supplied for me, and for proofreading the original text and offering insightful comments.

Andrea Povey for the fantastic cover photo, which sums up the book completely.

Christian Duck and the team at Amberley, with whom it has been a pleasure to work on this book. Finally to all my friends and family who have encouraged this endeveavour.

Notes

Introduction: The Killing of a King

1. See the genealogical table on page 7 for the lineage of the royal houses of Lancaster and York.

2. Nigel Jones' article in the *Daily Mail*, 26 September 2013. At the time of writing (December 2013) the site at Towton is under threat. The battlefield has been designated for use as a travellers' site. It would seem that the site of the bloodiest battle fought on English soil will vanish altogether.

3. In the medieval period verbal contracts of marriage were binding, therefore Edward's contract with Eleanor overrode his marriage to Elizabeth.

4. There is still a great deal of controversy about the fate of the Princes in the Tower. The skeletons of two young people that were found in the stairwell during renovation work could not have been the princes because of the age disparity. They are interred in Westminster Abbey but their remains have not been subjected to scientific analysis. There are many books on the subject of the princes and their fate, a few of which are listed in the bibliography.

5. Paul Murray Kendal, *Richard III* (London 1970), p. 261.

6. Translation: 'Judge not and defend my cause'.

7. W. Garner-Jones, *Welsh Nationalism and Henry Tudor*, pp. 32 and 33.

8. Polydore Vergil.

9. York Records, p. 218.

10. A halberd was a long pole axe, as depicted in the colour section.

11. Jean Molinet, *Chroniques de Jean Molinet* (Paris, 1828) p. 409.

12. I. and J. Lloyd-Williams, *Gwaith Guto'r Glyn* (Cardiff, 1939) pp. 263–4.

1 Gruffydd ap Nicholas: The Rise of the Raven (1430–1474)

1. See map of Wales.

2. A. D., Carr, *Medieval Wales*, p. 119.

3. The Welsh used the patronymic system for surnames, each son named after his father, i.e. Gruffydd (son of) Nicholas.

4. Huw Caer Llwyd (1431–1505) and Lewis Glyn Cothi (1420–81).

5. Henry Tudor's father died just after Henry's birth and so never saw his son.

6. Owain Glyndŵr declared himself Prince of Wales in 1400. The rebellion against the English lasted until 1416, by which time Glyndŵr was already dead.

7. See Fig. 2.

8. The office of sheriff.

9. R. A. Griffiths, *Rhys ap Thomas and His Family*, p. 14.

10. Griffiths, p. 15.

11. E. D. Jones (ed.), *Glyn Lewis Cothi*, 6 (Cardiff, 1984).

12. T. D. Lloyd, *Arch Camb.*, fourth series IX, (1878), p. 202–6.

13. *Life of Sir Rhys ap Thomas.*

14. *Ibid.*

15. A. L. Rowe, *Bosworth Field and the Wars of the Roses*, p. 204.

16. Reinstatement of the king.

17. Polydore Vergil, p. 155.

18. J. Balinger, *History of the Glyndŵr Family*, p. 27.

19. *Life.*

20. Griffiths, p. 35.

2 Rhys ap Thomas: The Man Who Killed Richard III (1474–1485)

1. Henry Rice, *Life of Sir Rhys ap Thomas*, was first published in its entirety in 1796 in the inaugural volume of the *Cambrian Register* and did not appear again in print until 1993 in R. A. Griffiths, *Sir Rhys ap Thomas and His Family* (Cardiff, 1993).

2. Lewis Caerleon did indeed serve the family and as a noted astrologer could well have cast Rhys's horoscope. Copies of horoscopes by Lewis Caerleon survive in Cambridge University Library, MS Ec. III 61 f.159ff, 108eff.

3. Griffiths, p. 35.

4. This poem is attributed to Rhys Nannor (1480–1513).

5. Paul Murray Kendal, *Richard III*, p. 205.

6. Griffiths, p. 37.

7. Kendal, p. 261.

8. *Ibid.*, p. 287.

9. *Ibid.*, p. 327–8.

10. Kendal, p. 272.

11. Griffiths.

3 The Road to Bosworth

1. *Life.*

2. For translation see Introduction, note 6.

3. Lewis Glyn Cothi.

4. Griffiths, p. 41.

5. *Life.*

6. Polydore Vergil, *English History*, p. 217.

7. *Ibid.*

8. *Ibid.*

9. *Ibid.*

10. I. and J. Lloyd-Williams, *Gwaith Guto'r Glyn* (Cardiff, 1939).

11. J. A. Buchan (ed.), Jean Molinet, *Chroniques 1476–1506* (Paris, 1827–8).

12. T. Penn, *The Winter King*, p. 10.

13. In A. L. Rowe, *Bosworth Field and the Wars of the Roses.*

4 The Red Rose Restored (1485–1499)

1. Vergil, *English History*, p. 217.

2. Griffiths.

3. Unattributed. Griffiths, p. 45.

4. *Croyland Chronicle.*

5. Lewis Glyn Cothi.

6. Stevens, *Music and Poetry in the Early Tudor Court* pp. 364–5 in Penn, p. 22.

7. Lewis Glyn Cothi.

8. Griffiths, 239.

9. *Ibid.*

10. Penn, p. 39.

11. Griffiths.

12. Penn, p. 30.

13. Griffiths, p. 244.

14. *Life.*

15. The priest mentioned could possibly be Lewis Caerleon.

5 Festivals and Farewells (1500–1509)

1. Edmund Tudor's tomb can be seen in St David's Cathedral, Pembroke.

2. Penn, p. 62.

3. *Life.*

4. Griffiths, p. 53.

5. *Ibid*, p. 87.

6. *Ibid*, p. 96.

7. Vergil, *English History*.

8. *Life*.

9. L.T. Smith, *Itinerary in Wales of John Leland* (London, 1906), p. 57.

10. *Ibid*., pp. 115–16.

11. *Life*.

12. *Life*.

13. *Life*.

14. Virgil, *Eclogues* III, pp. 108–10.

15. *Life*.

16. The chair and bed belonging to Rhys ap Thomas can be seen in St Fagan's Museum, Cardiff.

17. *Life*.

18. Griffiths, 85.

19. Catherine St John married Piers Edgecombe of Cothele House, Cornwall. She took with her a pair of chairs and the 'Cothele Testor', a large oak cupboard, which had belonged to her husband Gruffydd ap Rhys. The items still remain at the house, which is now owned by the National Trust.

20. Richard Pynson was a Fleet Street printer.

6 King of the Ravens (1509–1524)

1. *Life*.

2. 'Flower of the Welshmen', *Holishead's Chronicles* III, p. 576.

3. *Life*.

4. *Ibid*.

5. *Ibid*.

6. *Ibid*.

7. Griffiths, p. 57.

8. Anon.

9. *Life*.

10. An anonymous poem, the only one written in English. Griffiths says that the poet possibly comes from South West Wales and was in the entourage of Sir Gruffydd at the Field of the Cloth of Gold. Griffiths, p. 86.

11. The *Paston Letters*, a compilation of documents relating to the family, give a good explanation of how marriages were organised and arranged.

12. The ruins of the Hospitaller's church at Slebech can still be seen; for a description of the ruins and access to them see P. Davis and S. Lloyd-Fern, *Lost Churches of Wales and the Marches* (Alan Sutton, 1987).

13. Elis Gruffydd was a Flintshire chronicler. See Griffiths, p. 72.

14. NLW ms 1602 Df153 in Jones TCASFC XXIX (1939), p. 31.

15. Leland, *op. cit.*

16. See Chapter 6, note 20.

7 Presumption of the Raven (1525–1531)

1. George Cavendish, *The Life and Death of Cardinal Wolsey* (EETS 243, 1959).

2. See Chapter 6, note 13.

3. Small cargo boats.

4. PRO, SP1/54 f.119–20.

5. Griffiths, p. 99.

6. See Chapter 6, note 13.

7. LP, HVIII v 259.

8. LP, HVIII v 200.

9. LP, HVIII, VIII 230; cf CSP Span, V, part 1, p. 235.

10. Griffiths, p. 110.

11. Griffiths, p. 111.

8 Resurrection (1547–2013)

1. Griffiths, p. 123–4.

2. *Ibid.*, p. 131.

3. The Tesco store has now moved to another location in Carmarthen, but the Friary site in Llammas Street is still inhabited by retail outlets.

4. The BBC Radio 4 play *Echo of the Dragon* was aired in 1985 to mark the 500th anniversary of Bosworth Field. It was written by Rob Gittins, from an original idea, and research by Susan Lloyd-Fern

5. Philip Henslowe (1550–1616). According to his diary, the Admiral's Men bought the play *Henry of Richmond, Part Two* in 1599. This may have been the sequel to *Owen Tudor*, which was bought in the following January. Henry of Richmond charts the fall of Buckingham and the invasion of Henry Tudor. Sir Rhys ap Thomas was one of the leading characters in the now lost play.

Bibliography

Ashdown-Hill, J., *The Last Days of Richard III* (2012).

Ballinger, J. (ed.), *History of Glyndŵr Families* (Cardiff, 1927).

Buchan, J. A. (ed.), Jean Molinet, *Chroniques 1476–1506* (Paris, 1827–8).

Carr, A. D., *Medieval Wales* (London, 1995).

Chrimes, S. B., *Henry VII* (London, 1972).

Davis, N. (ed.), *Paston Letters and papers of 15th century*, 2 Vols (Oxford, 1971–6).

Davis, P. R. and S. Lloyd-Fern, *Lost Churches of Wales and the Marches* (Sutton, 1987).

Ellis, H., *Holinshed's Chronicles* Vol. III (London, 1808).

Ellis, H. (ed.), *Three Books of Polydore Vergil's English History* Camden first series, 29 (Camden Society, 1844).

Griffiths, R. A., *Sir Rhys ap Thomas and his Family: A Study in the Wars of the Roses and Early Tudor Politics* (Cardiff, 1993).

Jones, D., *The Plantagenets* (London, 2013).

Jones, N., *Daily Mail* (26 September 2013).

Jones, E. D. (ed.), *Glyn Lewis Cothi*, 6 (Cardiff, 1984).

Kendal, P. M., *Richard III* (London, 1972).

Lloyd, J. E. (ed.), *History of Carmarthenshire*, 2 Vols (Cardiff, 1935–9).

Lloyd, T. D., *Arch Camb.*, fourth series IX (1878).

Lloyd-Williams, I. and J., *Gwaith Guto'r Glyn* (Cardiff, 1939).

Penn, Thomas, *The Winter King* (London, 2011).

Rowse, A. L., *Bosworth Field and the Wars of the Roses* (1998).

Skidmore, C., *Bosworth and the Birth of the Tudors* (Orion, 2013).

Smith, L. T., *Itinerary in Wales of John Leland* (London, 1906).

Vaughan, R., *Philip the Good* (London, 1970).

Wilkinson, J., *The Princes in the Tower* (Amberley, 2013).

Index

Index

Richard III from Amberley Publishing

RICHARD III
David Baldwin

'A believably complex Richard, neither wholly villain nor hero'
PHILIPPA GREGORY

£9.99   978-1-4456-1591-2   272 pages PB 81 illus, 57 col

ANNE NEVILLE
Amy Licence

'Timely ... the real life of the daughter of Warwick the Kingmaker'
WI LIFE

£10.99   978-1-4456-3312-1   304 pages PB 30 col illus

CECILY NEVILLE
Amy Licence

£20.00   978-1-4456-2123-4   256 pages HB 35 illus

THE PRINCES IN THE TOWER
Josephine Wilkinson

£18.99   978-1-4456-1974-3   192 pages HB

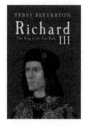

RICHARD III
Terry Breverton

£16.99   978-1-4456-2105-0   200 pages HB 20 col illus

RICHARD III: THE YOUNG KING TO BE
Josephine Wilkinson

£9.99   978-1-84868-513-0   352 pages PB 40 illus, 25 col

THE MYSTERY OF THE PRINCES
Audrey Williamson

'Brilliant and readable'
THE TRIBUNE

£9.99   978-1-84868-321-1   192 pages PB 40 col illus

MARGARET OF YORK
Christine Weightman

'Brings Margaret alive once more'
THE YORKSHIRE POST

£10.99   978-1-4456-0819-8   256 pages PB 51 illus

ALSO AVAILABLE AS EBOOKS
Available from all good bookshops or to order direct
Please call **01453-847-800**
www.amberleybooks.com

CLN 12.6.14

CAERLEON